"The vulnerability of the Northern C[
lessons for the wider Church; as so ofte1.
the 'outsider'. Those of us who minister in the North know this, and now we have research evidence that backs this up! COVID-19 has heightened the inequalities in our society, challenging the Church's current priorities for mission and ministry. The publication of *Fuzzy Church* is timely and valuable: there are lessons here for the whole Church and a clear mandate for investment in a 'failing' Northern Church because 'something is happening' here!"

— **Claire Dawson**, *Vicar of St Mary's Bramall Lane, Sheffield*

—

"Having been brought up in Kent, but spending most of my ministry in the North of England, I was greatly encouraged to read the reflections in *Fuzzy Church*. The authors have resisted the stereotypes of Northernness and offer a deft yet gentle enquiry into the distinctive nature of the 'fuzzy-edged' churches they have studied. Their use of organic imagery, their willingness to embrace nuance, their engagement with broad theological themes make for an interesting read. This book brings us through an examination of culture and context to ask, 'Can the churches of the North give us a clue to the transformation of the post-Christendom Church?'"

— **Barbara Glasson**, *President of the Methodist Conference, 2019–20*

—

"What a gift! A knotty, informed and passionate reflection on the complex North and what the good news of Jesus looks like *here*. Elli and Nigel have given us a helpful primer on contextual theology and some provocative pointers for mission but, more than that, reasons to be hopeful that post-Christendom church life can be adventurous, authentic, hospitable and, in partnership with the Spirit of God, that it can flourish."

— **Mark Powley**, *Principal, St Hild College*

"The 2016 book *Northern Gospel, Northern Church* raised important and pressing questions about the nature of the gospel in the North of England and how God's mission was finding expression there. This book, based on some well-designed and targeted qualitative research, assembles a set of substantial and illuminating responses to those questions, taking forward the discussion in informed ways. The authors quote the Brazilian Bishop Pedro Casaldáliga for whom 'the universal word speaks only dialect', and find how 'something is happening' in the neighbourhoods and villages of the North of England, something that manifests God's mission. The book provides an engaging object lesson in how churches in any region of the world, global North or global South, can seek out God's mission in the unique textures of their local life and find encouragement and inspiration in that. In the Christian tradition renewal and growth has nearly always come from the grass roots and margins of church life, which makes this book indispensable reading for anyone who cares about Christian mission."

— **Stephen Spencer**, *Director for Theological Education at the Anglican Communion Office, London*

—

"Nuanced, well researched, and wide-ranging, Rooms and Wort's book builds on *Northern Gospel, Northern Church* to investigate the crucial question of the relationship between the local church and the community it serves. At a time when the parish system is coming under increasing pressure, *Fuzzy Church* explores the importance of context in mission and evangelism. As a Northerner recently arrived in London, this book speaks to me of my roots, and challenges me to be 'taken by the hand' (Chapter 5) to explore what God is already doing here and now, so that I can join in the dance."

— **Catherine Pickford**, *Archdeacon of Northolt, Diocese of London*

"This is a simple but profound book that works on several levels: as a window into Northernness, an introduction to key topics and thinkers in mission studies, a group study for congregations, and an exploration of what it means to follow Jesus in ordinary congregational life. Though grounded in research and theology, ultimately, it is about discernment and faithful discipleship in the challenges and fuzziness of life."

> — **Kirsteen Kim**, *Paul E. Pierson Chair in World Christianity and Associate Dean for the Center for Missiological Research, Fuller Theological Seminary*

—

"'Don't be afraid of fragility', Pope Francis once said in a talk he gave at the Vatican. Nigel Rooms and Elli Wort could paraphrase this: 'Don't be afraid of fuzziness.' Don't be afraid of living with ambiguity in a post-Christendom and (hopefully soon) post-COVID-19 world. Don't be afraid, because 'something is happening' in the North, and it's worth our radical hope. *Fuzzy Church* is contextual theologizing and missiology at its best and written with humour and panache. The context is Northern England, but anyone who cares about the state and future of God's Church can read it with excitement and much profit."

> — **Steve Bevans SVD**, *Catholic Theological Union, Chicago*

—

"This fun, informing, transforming book joins excellent primary research with critical, post-colonial, and innovative missional practical theology. Although decidedly local in its research it uncovers the nuanced diversity of northern English culture that as a North American who has worked in local church development in the North of England clearly added powerfully to my appreciation of the differences between my culture setting and the deep similarities to the work of renewal after Christendom in my other work settings."

> — **Patrick Keifert**, *President and Director of Research, Church Innovations Institute, Saint Paul, MN*

Fuzzy Church

Gospel and Culture in the North of England

— NIGEL ROOMS & ELLI WORT —

Sacristy
Press

Sacristy Press
PO Box 612, Durham, DH1 9HT

www.sacristy.co.uk

First published in 2021 by Sacristy Press, Durham

Sacristy Limited, registered in England & Wales, number 7565667

British Library Cataloguing-in-Publication Data
A catalogue record for the book is available from the British Library

ISBN 978-1-78959-167-5

This book presents the findings and implications of qualitative field research in churches in the North of England where "something is happening".

Contents

Foreword

In the balmy days before COVID, I climbed on board a bus, made my way upstairs and sat on my favourite seat at the front. I turned to the young man I found myself sitting next to, smiled and made some bland comment about the weather. He looked at me in utter fear and panic, shifted as far away from me as he could and then moved to another seat at the next stop. I had forgotten I was in the south.

If you get on a bus in Burnley and fail to talk to the people around you, it is seen as a shocking act of incivility. In the south, the complete opposite is true. Even in a heaving bus or tube train, if you so much as acknowledge the existence of those into whose armpits your nose is being forced, people think you're dangerously insane or drunk. Or both.

It's a trivial example, but as someone who moves frequently between the north and the south it rather typifies the vast cultural difference between two regions of the same nation. And in recent years a wide combination of factors such as Brexit, austerity, COVID, HS2, the limp Northern Powerhouse project and the advent of the "Red Wall" Tory MPs have all served to heighten rather than play down those differences.

Which raises an interesting question for Christians. If these two regions of the same country are so different, should that have an impact on the way we live and proclaim the gospel? That was the question addressed in the book *Northern Gospel, Northern Church* which was published in 2016. The book was to my mind unconvincing, and I am grateful to Nigel Rooms and Elli Wort for exploring the question much more fully in this new work.

It comes at an important time. The Church of England, in common with some other denominations, has noticed that the disparities that go under the ill-defined expression "the north-south divide" are not just replicated but are magnified in the Church. Historic assets, clergy deployment and Sunday attendance are all massively skewed in favour of the south, and this has led to a laudable aim to invest more in the northern church, something expressed most clearly in funding streams from the Church Commissioners, especially Lowest Income Communities Funding and the Strategic Development Fund which together are pouring tens of millions of pounds into mission to the north.

LICF

But how best to invest? At the moment the answer appears to be that we are trying everything. Some dioceses and denominations are going through processes of restructuring and pastoral re-organization to have fewer, more "viable" churches with a more affordable level of clergy staffing. Some are staying faithful to the traditional parish and seeking to intervene only where there is weakness or failure. Some are trying the Resource Church model imported from London in which heavy investment is made in selected town centre churches which can then plant out. Some are trying a pioneering approach in which gifted leaders try to grow indigenous churches from scratch. Some are working ecumenically to replace the parish with mission units. Some are encouraging parishes to start new congregations which can reach out to those for whom Sunday morning is time for football or sleep.

The rich and detailed field which is such a feature of this book has much to offer these strategic questions. But there is more. Whilst we may be experimenting with every technique in search of the golden bullet, what we rarely stop to do is explore the theological and missiological approaches that lie behind them. Is the gospel a message, a person or a relationship? Do we import it from outside or find it already there, like the treasure buried in a field?

As I feared they might, Rooms and Wort struggle (with admirable and thoroughly northern honesty) to answer the core question about a northern gospel. The north (despite the clear cultural contrast revealed on the buses) is too hard to define and church life too varied and rich to find a clear answer to such a blunt question. Instead they pose new questions which arguably are much more fruitful. In particular they ask what the churches of the north, fragile as they may be, can teach the whole Church about what it means to participate in the mission of God. They raise rich and challenging dilemmas about the right relationship between the local church and the community it seeks to serve. And of course, drawn directly from their research, they introduce us to the novel concept of "Fuzzy Church".

But what they do above all is pose an acute challenge to the whole Church to think through the theologies that lie, often subconsciously, behind our evangelistic techniques and strategies. If we want to renew a nation in Christ, we need to know who He is.

+Philip Burnley

Acknowledgements

We would like to acknowledge the generous research grant from The Susanna Wesley Foundation <https://susannawesleyfoundation.org/> that made possible the field research on which this book is based. In particular, Sue Miller at the Foundation was enormously helpful in making the process of applying for and administering the grant smooth and, seemingly, effortless.

Similarly, we are immensely grateful to all those in northern church bodies who helped us identify the local churches we researched and everyone in them who gave of their time and energy so generously. We need too to thank Steve Bevans SVD for his support and advice throughout the project.

A note about referencing and style

All Bible quotations are from the New Revised Standard Version, unless otherwise stated.

We have decided, since we are emphasizing its importance, to capitalize the nouns North and Northernness while leaving the adjective northern uncapitalized. In quotations from other works, we will remain faithful to the original capitalization or non-capitalization.

As far as is possible we use Church when referring to the whole institution and church when writing about its local manifestation in a particular place.

Preface

We wanted to be right up front about the title for this book, since honestly it took until we were near the end of writing it before it emerged. However, we think this is entirely consistent with the nature of doing research, which is that one sets out with a hunch (a hypothesis is the technical term) or two, not really knowing where you will end up. We set out with some ideas about the relationship of faith and culture in the North, which soon fell away! We explain more about our research journey in the Introduction, but the first move or shift we had to make was from researching what we thought could be called "flourishing" churches in the North of England to simply churches where "something is happening". The implication of that phrase was that something new is happening in these places which hasn't really occurred in this way before, but that it was very fragile and couldn't be named as flourishing at all yet. "Something is Happening", however, made for a really dull title.

So, moving on, we were presenting the research findings in detail when preparing Chapter 4 and came across this quote from a leader in a set of rural churches in Yorkshire when asked about how people were coming to Christian faith there (i.e. "something was happening"):

> I think there's a bit of fluffy edges [at the church] though when I say people are coming to faith, it's quite hard to know when that is because there is no point at which they sign on the dotted line. But, but what we can see is people who didn't come to church, were not bothered about God, who now are and who will have conversations. So, I guess that's perhaps what we're talking about when we say coming to faith. There are not, not necessarily those overt signs but I, I, I think again it's a fuzzy edge about a few things, that it's about community and feeling part of something and belonging.

Some readers will be familiar with the study of "Ordinary Theology", which was inaugurated by Jeff Astley in a book of the same name published in 2002. The idea was to study what Christians with no formal theological education believed on the assumption that they too were theologians, just not trained ones. The word "ordinary" in the title of the book (and subsequent major studies) developed almost as a joke from an interviewee who participated in research in the sociology of religion conducted in London in the 1960s (2002: 45). The interviewer asked, "Do you believe in a God who can change the course of events on earth?" and the answer came back, "No, just the ordinary one." Astley says a lot more about his interpretation of the word "ordinary", but that is his starting point. So, in a similar fashion we are taking a word spoken by one of our respondents, and claiming it as a way of encapsulating the whole research project we undertook.

What we are going to claim is that fuzzy, especially at church, is a good thing. But we have to be a bit careful here. Fluffy and fuzzy are conflated in the quotation above. What we wish to avoid is any sense that fuzzy equals wishy-washy, without focus, grounding or intention. Quite the opposite, in fact. We are using fuzzy in the same way that management and leadership consultants use the term "fuzzy goal". Just put those two words into an internet search engine, and the results will be illuminating. Essentially a fuzzy goal is somewhere in between a very specific and boundaried goal that might actually turn out, when you got there, to not be where you wanted to be after all, and a goal that is so vague that you will have no idea if you have arrived at it or not. A fuzzy goal sets an intentional direction of travel without finally defining the outcome. In fact, this whole research project, as we noted above, could be described as the realization of some fuzzy goals we set out with.

The sending of the seventy (or seventy-two) disciples in Luke 10:1–12 is a good example of Jesus offering a fuzzy goal. There are some very specific instructions about *how* to go about the journey (carry no purse, no bag, no sandals, greet no-one on the road) and *what* to say in certain situations ("peace to this house", "the Kingdom of God has come near"), but beyond that almost anything could happen (and probably did). I suppose we don't like fuzzy because I suspect it requires faith and trust to live in the relative uncertainty it brings.

What we are therefore going to try and demonstrate in this book is the importance of fuzzy for churches where "something is happening" in the face of the inexorable decline and even death of mainstream churches in the North of England (and by extension elsewhere). We will claim first that, as our friend in Yorkshire had discovered, churches need fuzzy boundaries. Not hard boundaries to the outside, not no boundary at all, but fuzzy ones where one can't quite tell who is "in" and who is "out". We are going to blur and complexify the boundary therefore between the Church and the world and by extension faith and culture in the North—the very things we set out originally to research. We'll discover (again from our respondents) that if Jesus were to turn up today in the North, you might well sit beside him on the top deck of a bus, and perhaps you might or might not notice him. We will also claim that what happens in the worship of churches where something is happening is pretty fuzzy too. It is a mixing, a hybridization of many elements drawn from diverse sources locally and globally.

Fuzzy won't be the only thing a reader learns from this book, but we offer it in the title as it captures the spirit of what we have discovered. It is also a fun and even funny word and, as we have learnt to appreciate the humour to be found in northern culture, we use it here in the hope that reading our book will not be a dreary experience, but a happy one. Welcome to Fuzzy Church!

"Something's happening": Gospel and culture in northern churches

This book has its genesis in a day conference at Bishopthorpe Palace in 2013, when Nigel Rooms and Gavin Wakefield invited people from across the North of England to reflect on the place of the gospel in the North, and what our response to that gospel should be. From this day conference came the 2016 book of essays and contributions *Northern Gospel, Northern Church: Reflections on Identity and Mission*, edited by Nigel and Gavin, with a foreword from Archbishop Sentamu.

In that book, contributors wrestled with the idea of a northern gospel: the then Bishop of Sheffield, Dr Steven Croft, argued that there is one gospel, and one way of understanding that gospel. Nigel responded to Steven's paper, arguing instead that the relationship between gospel and culture is always dynamic, and that it might be possible to envisage a distinctively northern gospel.

Elsewhere in *Northern Gospel, Northern Church*, Catherine Pickford explored what it might mean to be Geordie and Christian, and Claire Dawson reflected on the gospel in Bootle. Gavin Wakefield discussed prominent stories and key themes in the history of the North, linking them to present concerns over the use of power and powerlessness, and the relationship of the North to the rest of England. John Wigfield asked whether the Book of Deuteronomy might offer a missiological framework to explore the inequalities of the North-South divide, and John Thomson explored Anglican mission in the light of Stanley Hauerwas' concern for churches to be aware of their distinctive Christian identity in contexts where their experience is often of fragility—a theme which definitely resonates with our research as presented in this book.

James Newcome discussed the development of reconciliation via a new foundation in Carlisle, and Stephen Spencer explored the role of the North in shaping the life and ministry of William Temple. Su Reid explicitly brought some of Temple's concerns up to date by reflecting on the lives of those who are poor and dependent on welfare, using Middlesbrough as a case study, and in a second essay, compared the historical and contemporary sense of marginality in the North and the biblical material on Samaritans at the time of Jesus.

David Goodhew discussed his research on the growth of new churches in the North East, and Matthew Porter wrote about praying for God's transformation of the North, describing the call to re-evangelize and to pray for the North. Michael Sadgrove explored the Northernness of Durham Cathedral and "mission with a North East accent" in a significant exploration of the links between mission and identity, and Mark Tanner reported on micromissions undertaken by students at Cranmer Hall, also in Durham. Mark Powley explored issues around the calling and deployment of clergy in the North, and Nigel ended the book by challenging the myth that "It's Grim up North".

In a review of the book, the Bishop of Burnley, the Rt Revd Philip North, expressed frustration with the level of engagement that a book of essays can have with the subject of gospel and culture (*CT* 29 April 2016):

> Whatever one might conclude about the contextual nature of evangelism, there is no doubt that, if we are to capture imaginations with the gospel, we need an intelligent, theological understanding of the issues that are specific to a particular place and culture to answer the questions that people are asking. A project on such a scale is, however, not patient of the short-essay format of this collection. Rooms needs to turn his chapter into a book.

Here then was a challenge to go deeper, which we have taken up in this research and hence the publication of this book.

Northern Gospel, Northern Church and its rich collection of essays begins a conversation and begs a question: *is* there a northern gospel, and if so, what is it? The Brazilian Bishop Pedro Casaldáliga wrote that "the universal word speaks only dialect" (Casaldáliga, 1978: 211): is it possible therefore to hear a gospel with a northern accent in our churches and communities?

We were also challenged by Ian Bradley's review of *Northern Gospel, Northern Church*, where he critiqued the book for being "filled with depressing statistics showing the north to be poorer, unhealthier and generally less confident and self-assured than the south", and for reinforcing rather than debunking the myth that it's "grim up North" (Bradley, 2017). There are, of course, significant areas of poverty in the Midlands, the South and West of England, in Wales, Scotland and Northern Ireland. However, the fact remains that much of the North does experience more deprivation than the South of England, and also that these are places where the good news of the gospel is experienced. We hope that this book will show what the good news looks like in such areas, but we cannot pretend that the North is something it is not, and we will explore its distinctiveness further in Chapter 2. We did, at one point, wonder about calling this book "Summat's 'Appenin'", in an attempt to characterize the particularity of the accented gospel in the North, but felt this might come over as caricature—a phenomenon we'll also return to in detail in Chapter 2.

At this point we should initially locate ourselves, though we'll need to say more about location later in the book, especially Chapter 6. We are both white, middle-class Anglican Christians, who have received high levels of education. Nigel is originally from the North but currently lives in the East Midlands; Elli is originally from the South but now lives in the North. We recognize that we are both "insiders" and "outsiders" in the churches and communities we are researching; the results of our research are shaped by the lenses that we bring to it.

Our enquiries are also shaped by the type of churches we researched. We focused on Anglican and Methodist churches: the original northern gospel research emerged from a Church of England conference, and we received generous funding for our investigations from the Methodist Susanna Wesley Foundation. This does mean that the findings of our research into a northern gospel come from and sit within established and traditional churches, but we hope that leaders of northern churches from other or no denominations will be able to test our theories and compare and contrast them against their own church experiences.

Our research and its method

In order to set out on our research journey into the question of faith and culture in the North, we needed to select some churches to study. We reasoned that if we were looking for a northern gospel, we needed to be looking in places where the gospel was taken seriously and being lived out in the lives of churches and communities, however that might look. It would have been wonderful to research in large numbers of churches and communities across the North of England, but that would have taken resources far beyond this project! So, we contacted key people and senior leaders in the Dioceses of the Anglican Northern Province and within the Methodist Church and asked them to give us the names of some churches we could research. We initially invited them to tell us about the churches in their patch that they thought were *flourishing* in their local communities, as this related to our starting research question (see below). However, we soon found there was a problem with this request: they, almost to a person, stumbled over the word "flourishing". We'd used the word "flourishing" to indicate we were looking for churches where something interesting was going on, where God was at work, where growth might be happening, where people may be discovering the "gospel", however conceived, for the first time. But the various bishops, missioners, archdeacons and communications officers we spoke to struggled with our description: to them, "flourishing" meant "successful". And the churches they felt where something was happening, where good news was being expressed, were not always "successful". These were churches that could often be fragile, struggling, on the knife-edge between "success" and "failure". This gave us a first, crucial insight into a northern gospel: whatever that gospel might look like, it might not look like "success", like bums on pews or lots of money in the collection plate.

In accordance with such feedback we changed what we asked our diocesan contacts, and asked them to tell us about churches where interesting things were happening, where they felt God might be at work.

We began to talk together about places where "something is happening", first as almost a joke and then more seriously as we entered into these rare and enriching spaces. Such churches didn't have to be new or have glamorous projects, but simply places where we might catch a glimpse of the Holy Spirit at work. This was clearly a more useful way of phrasing the question, as our contacts could think of plenty of churches where interesting things were happening. From these initial conversations with our Church body contacts, we were given details of forty-nine churches across the North. These were a mix of churches from East to West, in cities and in rural areas, in coastal and inland areas, in affluent and more deprived areas; they were big churches and small churches, Anglican and Methodist, evangelical and catholic by tradition.

Our research question and initial hypotheses

We began our research hoping to discover an authentic northern gospel, an expression of good news and being church that was particular to the North of England. We had been expecting that in line with Bishop Philip's question, we would see a theology which was specific to a place and culture, namely, the North of England. As Nigel argued in his chapter in *Northern Gospel, Northern Church*, "the gospel cannot exist apart from culture—just as, in fact, a heart cannot live and beat without a body" (Wakefield and Rooms, 2016: 37). However, as our research progressed, we discovered that we had been a bit naïve; we'll say more about this naivety in Chapters 2 and 4 when we explore Northernness and present the results of the research. We did not discover a northern gospel, partly because "the North" is not one simple thing which can be equated in some kind of straight line with the gospel. We explain more about the background to this "failure" in our initial hypothesis in Chapter 2 as it relates to the study of culture. There we also share some of the informal conversations we undertook with people who could shed light on Northernness, such as the historian Michael Wood, alongside church leaders and writers such as Rachel Mann. We found much more complexity in the North than we had anticipated, more particularity in each location, and much more diversity than could be summed up as a simple "northern gospel". However, in retrospect, we're glad that we started by looking for a "northern gospel" and feel our initial research question was an "excellent failure". That is, despite not working as we had expected, it occasioned a great deal of learning as we dealt with the aftermath of that "failure". Although we may not have started from the right location, the question led us in the right direction.

And as described above, we also found out that "flourishing" was not a useful category to start our research from. After we shifted our focus away from "flourishing" to "something happening", we formulated the research question as: "What good news is at the heart of churches where 'something is happening' within their communities in the North of England?" To begin to answer our research question, we firstly wanted to find out how northern our churches were. We could probably assume that all churches in the North would be distinctly northern, but what if they were led by people from the South or Midlands, or had a congregation made up of students from other regions? We needed to find out whether the churches' leadership teams came from the North, the wider region (like Cumbria or Humberside), or from the very community the church served. We wanted to know how each church saw itself, and how it thought its local community might view it from the outside in, as it were. We wanted to know if these churches were helping people come to faith, and if so, how.

In conversation with Nigel about the project, Steve Bevans, author of *Models of Contextual Theology* (2002), suggested that to get to the heart of a northern gospel we needed to focus on the person of Jesus. At an elemental level, we recognize that Jesus is the good news at the heart of the gospel: to understand what the good news in a community and church is, we needed to investigate who that church understood Jesus to be, since Jesus, we assumed, would be being "made flesh" in the life, faith and worship of that community. So, we knew we also needed to ask questions about how the people in the churches saw or, perhaps, better imagined, Jesus. We therefore devised a survey to be filled in online for each church that wished to participate.

The survey questions

We sent our initial forty-nine churches an online survey to fill in, and asked:

- How local, regional or northern is your leadership team and congregation? Completely, mostly, a bit or not at all?
- What is your church's mission statement, or vision statement, if you have one?
- Are people discovering Christian faith afresh for themselves in your church? Regularly, occasionally, very occasionally, or not at all?
- Do these people "stick" in the church after professing faith?
- Have you any sense of what is enabling people to find faith with you?
- How do you perceive the relationship between your church and your wider local community, on a scale from completely cold/closed to completely warm/open?
- When doing things in the community, does the initiative come from the church or the community, or a mixture of both?
- How do you think the people outside church and in your community would describe you as a church?
- Thinking of how people in your church relate to Jesus what five words would you use to describe Jesus? Or, to put it another way, who is the Jesus people are worshipping at your church—what five words come to mind?

We finally asked if the church would be happy for us to come for a research visit.

Early results
Of the forty-nine churches (forty-four Anglican and five Methodist) we invited to fill in our survey, eighteen responded. This, we felt, was a healthy, if not fantastic, 37 per cent response rate which could represent our chosen constituency of northern churches where something was happening.

78 per cent of our respondents said their church leadership was completely or mostly local, and 94 per cent said their church leadership was completely or mostly northern or regional. All respondents said their church congregation was completely or mostly local and northern. The vision statements of our respondents' churches included "Nobody's

Perfect—Anything's Possible", "To know Jesus and make Him known", and "I came that they may have life, and have it abundantly". Three churches mentioned the name of their parish or community in their statement, and three either didn't have a mission statement or were reviewing it.

All our respondents said people were coming to faith in their churches: 44 per cent saw people regularly coming to faith, and 56 per cent saw people occasionally coming to faith. 44 per cent of respondents said these new Christians were regularly sticking in their church after professing faith, and 50 per cent said these people were occasionally staying in church after professing faith: 94 per cent in total. When describing what was enabling people to come to faith, our participants described "strong sense of family, belonging and welcome", being an inclusive church, encouraging people to ask questions, and "fresh starts and a new hope". Three respondents mentioned the Alpha course, one mentioned Fresh Expressions of worship, and one mentioned funerals, weddings and baptisms.

95 per cent of our respondents said that the relationship between their church and the community was somewhat or completely warm and open. When doing things with the community, 55 per cent of our respondents said that the initiative came mainly from the church, and 44 per cent said that the initiative came mainly from negotiating between church and community. When describing how the people outside the church might speak about the church, our participants mentioned being "friendly", "welcoming", "lively", "at the heart of the community", and a practical help to people: one participant said, "literally a quotation I hear from time to time [is], 'Yours is the Church that really helps people'". When our participants shared the five words they used to describe Jesus, the most common one was "friend", with ten mentions. "Love" or "loving" came joint second with "saviour", at seven mentions each. "Lord" was used by five participants, and "teacher" by four. We'll examine these findings in more detail in Chapter 4.

These questions, and our participants' results, helped us with a clear steer on some issues. The churches where our research contacts felt "something was happening", where God might be at work, were churches where people were coming to faith, and often staying in the church. These were churches where there was a strong relationship between the community and the church, and often where church and community would work together. These were churches with a strong sense of "localness" and "Northernness" in both the leadership and the congregation. These results also started to give us tantalizing glimpses of what a northern gospel in these churches might look like: it might be about abundant life, where anything was possible. It might be a gospel where Jesus was seen as a friend, as loving, as a saviour.

Field visits
We also asked our participants if they would be willing for a researcher to come and visit them for a more detailed field visit: most said yes. Over late 2018 and early 2019, we visited seven churches: again, these came from across the breadth of northern England, in cities and in rural areas, in coastal and inland areas, in affluent and more deprived areas; they were big churches and small churches, evangelical and catholic in tradition. Four of the churches were Anglican, one was Methodist and the two others had some ecumenical connection between a mainly Anglican foundation and the Methodist and other churches. We would like to take this opportunity to thank these churches—their leadership teams, the new Christians who met with us, and their welcoming congregations—for allowing and enabling us to research among them. In this book we have done our very best to anonymize the contribution our research respondents made to us, while telling the reader something about the places we visited. In the Appendix is a list of these seven churches from A to G with some brief information about them and their context, but not enough, we trust, to identify them. Normally when we quote from our research data in this book, we will say which church the quotation comes from.

Our research with these churches had four elements: an area visit, a focus group with the leaders (in all seven churches), a focus group with new Christians (in five churches, it proved not possible in two), and our "participant observation" in worship. The area visit was a guided tour of the church's patch, to help us get an overall "sense" of the community and the context. We tried to create a picture of what is within the local "horizon" of the church and its members, where the "edges" of the community might be, and where the people in the church live. We asked the person who showed us around the area to point out to us the important places we should know about: anywhere that the church or its members have a relationship with and other places of local significance in their own right.

In the leadership focus groups, we asked to speak to people the church felt were part of their leadership team. We asked them how local, regional or northern they felt (referring throughout to the survey answers they had filled in), and whether it mattered where the leadership comes from. We asked if the congregation were local, regional or northern, and whether it was important to account for the localness or otherwise of the church members, and how that affected the way they operated. We asked why people were finding faith with the church, and what was working for them: and out of all this what would they say was the gospel, here and now amongst them. We talked about the relationship between church and local community, what might make people in the community be "warm" to them, and what, if anything, might "put them off" them? We talked about the five words they had used to describe Jesus in their online survey: were these words that the congregation would agree with? What other words might be appropriate? We asked, "If Jesus walked your streets today what would he be like?"

In the groups with new Christians, or people who had returned to faith after a long time away, we used pictures to start our conversations. We provided twelve different pictures of Jesus from different cultures around the world. There was Holman Hunt's picture of Jesus as the light of the world, a Chinese depiction of Jesus among the little children, and a Native American picture of Jesus and the Sacred Heart. We included pictures of Jesus as a white-skinned man, and a picture of Jesus as a crucified woman, or Christa. We also included pictures which might have particularly northern resonance: a fisherman on a North Atlantic trawler, the Angel of the North, a picture of Jesus in the Blackpool illuminations, and a man dressed as Jesus in a football crowd, holding up a sign in support of the team's manager. We asked our participants to select the picture that reminded them most of Jesus and tell us why they chose that one.

We found that pictures are a really useful way of starting conversations about faith with people. Using visual research methods can access more information, and different kinds of information, than can be gained in an interview using words alone. Douglas Harper argues that one reason for this may be due to the evolution of the human brain:

> The parts of the brain that process visual information are evolutionarily older than the parts that process verbal information ... Images evoke deeper elements of human consciousness than do words; exchanges based on words alone utilize less of the brain's capacity than do exchanges in which the brain is processing images as well as words (Harper, 2002: 13).

Rosalind Pearmain describes the use of images as generating a "bigger space" for talking about spiritual experience (Pearmain, 2007: 80). Visual research methods not only tap a deeper level of human understanding but also create a wider arena in which to discuss religion and spirituality.

We also wanted to discover how our participants might have been changed by becoming Christians. We asked if when they started coming to church, there were any things they felt they had to give up or stop doing. Were there any things they felt they had to pick up, or start doing? If they were telling a friend about their experience of being a Christian, what would they say?

We took part in our churches' main worship services. We wanted to write what is known as a "thick description": to capture our experience of worship in rich detail, paying attention to both what happened in the service and when, but also when the congregation were engaged or disengaged, the emotional feel of the worship and congregations as it ebbed and flowed, and who led which parts of the service. We wanted to pay particular attention to local voice in the sermon and prayers, both in terms of accent and language, and any references to the local community or the wider world.

When we had transcribed the focus groups and written up our field visit notes this amounted to just over 100,000 words of qualitative text data in total.

How we looked at our data

After reading and re-reading our records of these visits, we found some overarching themes emerged that were common to the seven churches we visited. We analysed these themes using a programme called Nvivo, which helps researchers analyse qualitative data. We analysed the most common words used by our participants on the different themes, and whether particular words were used by church leaders or people new to Christianity. We paid particular attention to how church leaders and new Christians described Jesus, and how our new Christians found faith.

What we found out . . . and presenting our findings in this book

Our findings from this research will inform the rest of this book. In the first chapter, we're going to dive a bit deeper into the idea we mentioned at the start of this chapter, that "the universal word speaks only dialect", and ask how it might be possible for a northern gospel to exist (Casaldáliga, 1978: 211). In Chapter 2, we're going to look at what the North actually is, and why that might matter. In the third chapter, we will examine the current religious climate in Britain, and what the gospel might look like in northern churches in a post-Christian country. In Chapter 4, we're going to get into the meat of what is happening in our churches and why, and what the good news looks like in the North of England, all based on presenting data from the field research. Chapter 5 will be an imaginative description of the northern church, drawing together what we found from our visits to our seven churches, and where we saw something happening. In Chapter 6, we're going to suggest what a contemporary northern contextual theology might look like, and in Chapter 7, we'll look theologically at where and how God is at work in northern culture.

We thought some advice on reading the book might be helpful as sometimes starting at the beginning and reading through to the end is not the best way. A good place to start, after this Introduction, might be in Chapters 4 and 5—since this presents the heart of the research. Chapters 1 to 3 fill in the background to the research and some readers may be familiar with aspects of that, particularly Chapters 1 and 3 and prefer to skip over those. The final two chapters address the implications of the research from different theological perspectives where we hope to make make an original contribution, building on our findings.

We both discussed together all the chapters and own together what we have written in the whole book. We did though each initially take responsibility for certain chapters and write them separately, and some readers might wish to know that Nigel wrote Chapters 2, 4 and 6, and Elli Chapters 1, 3 and 7, while we both built up the picture presented in Chapter 5 and developed the Introduction here.

In each chapter, we want you to be able to relate these findings to your own church, whether you are in the North or South of England, in Wales, Scotland or Northern Ireland, or in fact elsewhere in the world—we think our contextual findings might have an appropriate universal applicability. If you're in the North, we'd be really interested to know if our theories and theologies sound familiar to you. If you're somewhere else in the UK, it would be fascinating to ask whether our findings are particular to the North, or whether they have resonance with communities in your area: have we found a northern gospel, or is it bigger than that? If you're in another country, especially one with a legacy of colonialism, are any of our findings recognizable in your context? We'll be helping you think about some of these things with questions at the end of each chapter. So, to start off your thinking, you could ask yourself some of the same questions we asked our churches in our online survey:

- How local, regional or northern (you could replace northern with whatever overarching name is given to your context) are your leadership team and congregation? Completely, mostly, a bit or not at all?
- How do you perceive the relationship between your church and your wider local community, on a scale from completely cold/closed to completely warm/open?
- When doing things in the community, does the initiative come from the church or the community, or a mixture of both?
- How do you think the people outside church and in your community would describe you as a church?

- Thinking of how people in your church relate to Jesus what five words would you use to describe Jesus? Or, to put it another way, who is the Jesus people are worshipping at your church—what five words come to mind?

It is also appropriate that we finish each chapter with questions because we know that any work of contextual theology (or more broadly practical theology) like this research never really ends, it just raises more questions. It has a cyclical or spiral shape and movement. We sincerely hope therefore, this isn't the last word on contextual theology in the North of England, neither can we claim it is a complete contemporary word on the subject. There are omissions we have made for the sake of focus, such as, for example, any engagement in-depth with the UK government's interest in the so-called "Norther Powerhouse" and other responses and calls for "levelling up" the economic divide in England. The research also took place wholly before the COVID-19 pandemic, and while the associated lockdown has given time for writing this book, we also know that we haven't engaged with the implications for local churches of the new world post-COVID-19 that we now live in. We are confident, however, that the *principles* we elucidate here are workable in this new world. Overall then, we trust that others may take up the baton from us and develop our work where we fall short.

CHAPTER 1

God, gospel, context and culture

Our research behind the specific research question we took to the churches where "something is happening" contains a deeper question about how we can discover God at work in the North of England today. In this chapter, we want to establish the basis on which we can connect the activity of God to the gospel of Jesus Christ set in a specific culture and context. Ever since the call of Abraham in Genesis 12 and the dream God gave Jacob at "Bethel" in Genesis 28 through to the birth of the Christ in Bethlehem, God has been calling to us out of specific places, cultures and *' out of '?* contexts. We believe God is still calling to us from the North of England and inviting us to find out what's going on. In the Introduction to this book, we quoted the Brazilian Bishop Pedro Casaldáliga's statement that "the universal word speaks only dialect" (Casaldáliga, 1978: 211). That's a similar idea: that God speaks to us in our own specific languages and culture. In this chapter, we're going to start to look into how that might be possible, and how God can call to us out of our context.

How can we know about God and the gospel?

To start, we need to look at how we can understand anything at all about God and the gospel. For generations, Anglicans and Methodists have used three or four sources to understand God and the gospel: scripture, tradition, reason and experience. In the Anglican tradition, this dates back to the work of the sixteenth-century priest and theologian Richard Hooker, who argued that scripture, tradition and reason were the bases of authority for the Church of England. In Hooker's time, the principle of looking to scripture and tradition was pretty well established within the Church; it was Hooker's insistence that people could also deduce the existence and nature of God by starting with the created world and the human mind that was more radical. These three sources of understanding about God are often referred to as the three-legged stool: the idea being that you need all three legs of scripture, tradition and reason to be able to know about God. If you only rely on one or two sources, your theology could become unstable and tip over. The classical Anglican position for centuries was that you need three legs, and to go to all three sources, to be able to be secure in your understanding of God.

In the eighteenth century, John Wesley added a fourth leg to this stool, or a fourth source of understanding about God: experience. Pentecostals and charismatics have reinforced the importance of this source since the beginning of the twentieth century. Wesley argued that you could also understand about God from your own personal experience. His famous quote about feeling his heart "strangely warmed" by the presence of God points to the way he understood God from within his own experiences. With Wesley's insertion of experience into the sources of understanding about God, these four sources (scripture, tradition, reason and experience) became known as the Wesleyan or Methodist Quadrilateral. This phrase always puts me in mind of some type of folk or ceilidh dance, and that's perhaps not a bad way of thinking of the Quadrilateral: it's dancing with these four sources to find the truth about God. And, like the analogy of the three-legged stool, in the Quadrilateral you need to dance between all four partners for the dance to work.

This idea of the dance also puts us in mind of Steve Bevans and Roger Schroeder's description of God as a dance. They describe how God is always moving, never static, how "God in God's deepest identity is a relationship, a communion". They describe how God's identity and life in communion:

> . . . spills out into creation, healing and sanctifying, calling all
> of creation, according to its capacity, into that communion, and
> once in that communion, sending that creation forth to gather
> still more of it into communion. It is as though God as such is a
> dance (a great conga line, one might imagine) moving through

the world, inviting the world—material creation, human beings—
to join in the dance (Bevans & Schroeder, 2011: 10).

If we want to join in God's dance of relationship throughout creation, we may find it helpful to dance between different sources to understand more about God and that dance.

We recognize that some readers will not normally go to tradition, reason or experience as ways of understanding about God. You may believe that we only need scripture to know about God and the gospel. But without tradition, experience and reason, we argue firstly that scripture is hard to decipher. The canon we know as the Bible today was only agreed on as a series of books in the fourth century: we owe a debt of gratitude to the faithful Christians of the early churches for gathering these texts together and deciding through the Holy Spirit what should form the canonical scriptures. And in subsequent centuries, we owe other Christians our thanks for translating the Bible into our native languages and sharing the scriptures across the world. We simply would not have access to scripture if it wasn't for Christians throughout the centuries. And this is part of what it is to learn about God through tradition. The word tradition is often taken to mean traditional ways of doing church, with old fashioned language and out-of-date ways. But we like to quote Jaroslav Pelikan on this: "Tradition is the living faith of the dead, traditionalism is the dead faith of the living" (Pelikan, 1984: 65).

So, if you, the reader are someone who goes to scripture first to understand about God, we are certainly not saying there's anything wrong with that! We all have a source that we go to first, and this is good. But it can help us to be aware which of the legs of the stool, or areas of the dance, we are weaker in. It can help our understanding of God to strengthen those areas, as well as taking the full richness from our preferred method of knowing God.

In this book, we argue that we can learn more about God and the gospel by paying attention to how God is working in different contexts. But, if this is the case, where does context fit in to the sources of knowing about God mentioned above? We might see context as another leg of the stool, or partner in the dance of knowing God: that is, as another source of theology. Or, we could understand it as an aspect which cuts across scripture, tradition, experience and reason, shaping how those sources inform our understanding of God, and this is the position we will take.

Context and scripture

When we go to scripture, there's often an assumption that we read the same verses in the same way. We assume that scripture is a central truth around which Christians across history and across the globe can gather. But if we look at scripture through the lens of contextual theology, we can realize that our understandings of scripture can be more complex than this. A simple example is wondering what Inuit people, living in permanently frozen conditions above the Arctic Circle, make of Jesus, "the lamb of God".

A more serious example of the relationship between context and scripture is demonstrated through liberation theology. It's also worth reminding ourselves of liberation theology as a way of understanding about God at this point, as contextual theology was born from liberation theology. Liberation theology was a product of the 1960s in Latin America, when populist and socialist movements in Argentina, Brazil and Mexico inspired Roman Catholic churches across the continent to engage closely with poor urban and rural people in their communities (Boff & Boff, 1987). Christians began to stand in solidarity with the poor and create "base worshipping communities" in deprived and oppressed areas (Boff & Boff, 1987: 67). This change by Latin American churches, from allying themselves with people in positions of authority to allying themselves with oppressed people, began receiving official support from the wider Roman Catholic churches with the Second Vatican Council (1962–65). This tied into similar movements from Christians across the world in the latter half of the twentieth century, as churches began listening to feminist and womanist theologies, African and North American black theologies, Dalit theology from India, Minjung theology from Korea, Palestinian theologies, and many more. Oppressed people across the world started to be listened to by those in positions of authority.

Liberation theology was inspired by, and led to, distinct ways of reading the Bible. An influential book at the time in South America was *Liberación y Libertad (Liberation and Liberty)* by José Severino Croatto (1973). Croatto saw the Exodus from Egypt as a crucial element in scripture: not only as an example of how God could liberate people from slavery, but also the foundational event of the Bible which explained the prophets, psalms, wisdom literature, and a good part of the New Testament (Andiñach & Botta, 2009: 4). Croatto and his fellow liberation theologians understood that in Exodus, God had liberated the slaves who called out in pain to God, and asked whether God could do the same for the poor in Latin America in the twentieth century. From this reading of the Old Testament came the understanding that Christ brings liberation and makes "humankind truly free" (Gutiérrez, 1973: 25). For the Church to be allied to the gospel of the liberating Christ, it had to be allied with the poor and stand with oppressed people.

In the case of liberation theology, we can see how the context of poverty across a continent affected how its Christians read the Bible. Robert Schreiter, an American Roman Catholic theologian, describes how context influences our reading of scripture:

> In the midst of grinding poverty, political violence, deprivation of rights, discrimination and hunger, Christians move from social analysis to finding echoes in biblical witness in order to understand the struggle in which they are engaged or to find direction for the future (Schreiter, 1985: 14).

Schreiter argues that when contexts are allowed to speak into how Christians understand scripture, people become:

> . . . genuinely and intimately coupled with the saving work of God. The energies that are released, the bonds of community and of hope that are forged, the insight into the divine revelation received and shared have already enriched the larger Christian community immediately and have challenged the older churches to a more faithful witness (Schreiter, 1985: 15).

Schreiter is saying that if we allow our context to help us read the Bible, we can understand more about God, and become more closely aligned with God's mission for the Church and world today.

Context and tradition

We suggested above that tradition is the sum total of what Christians have handed on to each other across time; the living faith of the dead. If we view tradition like this, it's easy to see how different contexts can shape tradition. Andrew Walls imagines an alien researcher from outer space studying Christianity on earth, who visits Jerusalem in 37 CE, Nicea in 325 CE, Ireland in the 600s, London in the 1840s, and Lagos in 1980. This space visitor would see Christians who are thinking about and doing very different things: law, obedience and sharing communal meals in Jerusalem in 37 CE, an intellectual concern with metaphysics and theology in Nicea in 325 CE, the desire for holiness via ascetic practices in Ireland in the 600s, activism and the involvement of faith in all aspects of society in London in 1840, and the power of preaching and healing in Lagos in 1980 (Walls, 1996: 1–6). This space visitor would notice that Christianity looks very different in each context of time and place.

However, if you come from a more catholic point of view, you may have a more formal view of what tradition is. You may understand the pronouncements and decisions of the Church across the centuries as having authority and wisdom about the nature of God. The Church of England as it exists today is "episcopally led and synodically governed" and looks to its bishops and councils to decide on policy and positions. Although each parish has its degree of autonomy, the Church's official position on issues such as sexuality are governed centrally. In the Methodist Church, the Conference and committees such as the Faith and Order Committee decide on matters of policy. So, how can we balance the idea of orthodox tradition coming from central figures and groups throughout the centuries with the idea that God can act in different contexts? How can local and newer theologies be reconciled to the wider tradition?

Schreiter, who we encountered earlier talking about liberation theology, has identified four big issues when we allow context and tradition to encounter each other:

- the desire for unity in the midst of diversity
- the possibility of syncretism and dilution of the Christian message
- the varying emphases put on differing elements of the tradition
- and how and when tradition should challenge local theology (Schreiter, 1985: 102–3).

2 way

Despite these potential questions, Schreiter does not squash the idea that we can understand God through our local contexts, and that this understanding might look different to the knowledge of God that we receive from traditional Church theology. Instead, he encourages his readers to see Church tradition as "a series of local theologies, closely wedded to and responding to different cultural traditions", that tradition itself was once generated within a local context and is shaped by that context (1985: 93). He argues that local theologies must engage with tradition to be truly Christian, but that we should also enable churches across the world to develop their local theologies, especially those churches which have traditionally not had a voice within global Christianity. Schreiter reminds us that these churches are not trying to dilute or avoid aspects of the tradition; there is a deep desire to remain truly faithful to the apostolic tradition and to be themselves faithful witnesses to the gospel in their own circumstances. However, the wider church must remember that God can reveal Godself to all people. Schreiter reminds us that theology is not the preserve of academic theologians or older, Western churches: theology can come out of the youngest of churches and Christians. But to be able to wrestle with issues like unity and syncretism, local theologies and traditional theologies must be in continual dialogue with one another, on an equal level. Traditional theology must be able to ask questions of local theology, and local and newer theologies must be able to ask questions of traditional theology as an equal partner.

Context and reason

The idea of reason as a source of understanding for God relies on the idea that we can use our rational faculties, our thinking skills, to understand more about God. Howard Stone describes reason as "taking care with how we think about things" (Stone, 2006: 53). He describes how:

> The precision of formal logic and mathematics is sometimes held up as the ideal, and some theologians have made attempts to model theology along the lines of the "hard" or social sciences, following the scientific method of reasoning and seeking equally assured results. Other theologians, however, point out that matters of faith are not rightly understood in scientific terms. They suggest that the scientific method is not as certain as it is often reputed to be. They urge theologians to reason well using means other than those of scientists (Stone, 2006: 54).

This helps us be aware that there is no one thing that is accepted as a universal way of thinking about things: our context will always affect how we use reason, and how we understand the very idea of knowledge itself.

The Asian American theologian Courtney Goto makes this point in her book *Taking on Practical Theology* (2018). She imagines a Korean American researcher, who she names Kim, writing an article about the practices of faith in a Korean American church:

> She has in mind a particular situation as the focus of her study, but she is at a loss as soon as she tries to analyze it. On one hand, she has a knowledge base of communal memories, personal experiences, and values that she has acquired by being born into the Korean American community. Kim has words for some of what she knows but not all. Her lived experiences inform what she knows of the situation that she is researching. On the other hand, most of the concepts, theories, and conversation partners that are common to rhetorical spaces in the field do not speak easily or directly to her situation or her culture. She is faced with a familiar dilemma: How do I accurately and authentically

describe and analyze this problem when I must translate much
of what I know into concepts and categories foreign to those I am
examining (and foreign to me)? (Goto, 2018: 47)

In this example, Kim's knowledge of her community and church is
profound, but the very way that this knowledge lives within her cannot
be translated into "reasonable" concepts that could be analysed by non-
Korean American theologians. Their very categories of thought (what
Goto refers to as the "rhetorical spaces in the field") are alien to those of
the community in which Kim worships and researches, and vice versa
(2018: 47).

Goto also reminds us that there is often a hierarchy of thought, with
its own patterns of power and privilege at work in such situations. As a
member of a minority group in the world of academic theology, Kim
must write up her research in a way that the gatekeepers of that world
find accessible and relevant to their way of thinking:

> . . . her task [Kim's] is no less than making the unfamiliar familiar
> to those in dominant groups, which involves some conformity
> on Kim's part. Though much will be lost in translation, for Kim
> it seems there is no alternative, since not translating leaves her
> research problem unintelligible and uninteresting—and thus
> irrelevant—to researchers and scholars. It would be easier for
> Kim not to theorize her community's situation or not to express
> her experience as an Asian American woman (and some people
> in her place don't). Her work has a greater chance of being
> understood (and published) the more she thinks, writes, and
> acts like a white scholar (Goto, 2018: 48).

Our contexts, with their own worlds of thought and experiences, will not
only shape what we understand reason and knowledge to be, but also be
part of a wider setting where some people's understandings of knowledge
and reason are less valued than others.

Context and experience

As we mentioned above, it was the founder of Methodism, John Wesley, who introduced many Christians to the idea that a person's own experiences could teach them about God. Wesley's own story has a wonderful example of how experience can help people know about God. Wesley had been ordained as a priest in the Church of England, and took his faith seriously, but his life was transformed by an experience in 1738 when he was thirty-five. He was at a talk where someone was preaching on Luther's *Preface to the Romans*, on the change that God can work in someone's heart, when, as Wesley said, "I felt my heart strangely warmed" (Davey, 1985: 10). He had known God in his head, but this experience of warmth, of God drawing near, made God real in a way that Wesley had not known before. The Methodist website describes how Wesley's legacy "particularly stresses the importance of our own experience of God's grace working in our lives. We gain wisdom and maturity from life experience, especially when we pray and reflect about our story with other Christians" (The Methodist Church, n.d.).

Stone describes how all of life and faith is a matter of experiencing:

> Every moment is a moment of experience with bodily, sensory, intellectual, emotional, and spiritual aspects: waking up, going to sleep, reading a good novel or the Bible, voting, dreaming, resisting bigotry, cleaning up the house, even breathing. The life of faith embraces the totality of our life experiences. And although the scriptures hardly ever call them experiences, this is the umbrella term used by theologians for the varied encounters with God, and for the awareness of God that comes through faith to the people of Israel, New Testament Christians, and to us today. In this sense, experiences of God are indispensable resources for theology (Stone, 2006: 55).

And of course, as with reason, our own particular contexts will shape how we experience and therefore how we imagine and relate to God. Courtney Goto makes another important point for people (like us, the authors of this book) researching faith communities. She reminds us that when we research context, we need to not only look out at the context we are studying, but inside ourselves and to the experiences and contexts that have formed who we are and our understandings of God (Goto, 2018: xvi). This is why we described ourselves in the introduction to this book as white, middle-class and university educated. These things will inevitably affect both how we research, and how we understand God. Our understandings of God have been shaped by our family backgrounds, where we have gone to church and the sort of churches we have attended, the people we have worked alongside and the way that we pray. When we research, the experiences that formed us will come into relation with the contexts we are studying. Goto reminds us that power and privilege will always play a part in this relationship (Goto, 2018: 100). We are the ones telling the story of the churches we researched, we are the ones publishing a book: we have an ability to be heard which comes in some part from our university education, our middle-class-ness, our whiteness. The way we see and write about both God and the context of the Church in the North of England is shaped by our own experiences and contexts.

So far, we've been looking at how we can understand God and the gospel (how we do theology) by looking at the *sources* for understanding God. Elaine Graham, Heather Walton and Frances Ward suggest a different way of theologizing, of understanding and talking about God, by looking at *methods*: asking *how* we do theology (Graham, Walton and Ward, 2005). The difference is clarified by comparing doing theology with making a chocolate cake. When you want to make a chocolate cake, you need a recipe. A recipe has both a set of ingredients and the method of how to make the cake. You could compare the sources of knowing about God: scripture, tradition, reason and experience; the three-legged stool or the Wesleyan Quadrilateral, with the ingredients you need for your cake (without pushing the analogy too far context might be like the different kinds of flour, sugar, chocolate etc. that you could use). Graham, Walton and Ward remind us we also need to focus on the methods we use to do theology, just as a recipe also has the method of baking the cake.

Graham, Walton and Ward categorize seven ways that people do theology, seven methods that people use to understand God and the gospel: first *theology by heart*, where "God is experienced as immanent, personal and intimate, speaking through the interiority of human experience";

second *speaking in parables*, where the "authoritative narrative of scripture is augmented and challenged by the voices of alternative experiences"; third *telling God's story*, where scripture is authoritative and Christian identity is "shaped around God's story as found in biblical narrative" and "the world stands in judgement under the power of that revelation". The fourth method, *writing the body of Christ*, takes the experiences of the community of faith as the "raw material of theological reflection"; fifth, *speaking of God in public*, is where "theological reflection occurs via a process of conversation or correlation between Christian revelation and surrounding culture"; sixth, *theology-in-action*, is where God is seen as "active in history, which is ushering creation towards an ultimate vision of redemption" (their version of liberation theology); and finally *theology in the vernacular*, where "the gospel finds expression across cultural differences of historical or geographical context" (2005: 14).

It is the last of these that we follow in this book and is comparable to Robert Schreiter's work quoted above. Contextual theology acknowledges that learning about God looks different in each different context, and different contexts need to be in conversation with each other to learn more about God. For example, White people need to learn from Black theologies, men need to learn from feminist theologies, and European churches need to learn from African churches. In this tradition of theology, we are bringing the churches of the North of England into a global conversation and asking what we can understand about God from learning about this context.

What do we mean when we talk about context and culture?

It will probably help at this point to be very clear what we mean when we talk about "context", and what we mean by "culture". Courtney Goto rightly criticizes her fellow theologians for not defining these words enough: she makes the point that theologians often treat "context" as a sign, a word with a transparent meaning which is clear and unambiguous, and therefore we all "know" what it means (Goto, 2018: 8). Goto instead suggests looking at "context" as a symbol, with a range of meaning and importance to different people. She also discusses four ways in which theologians define context: the background to, the circumstances that shed light on, or the story behind the subject the theologian is discussing, or the various circumstances of a place and time. Goto describes the latter definition of context as "a particular place time [that] has its own tightly woven historical/cultural/religious/aesthetic/political economy that resists being separated into parts" (Goto, 2018: 89).

The word "woven" here also helps us with a picture that might help us understand context more. The word "context" comes from the Latin words *textere*—to weave, and *con*—together. So "context" means to weave together. Goto argues that:

> . . . to consider context involves weaving together a complex picture of a practice of faith, situation, or problem under investigation. It brings to mind the challenging labor of untangling, combing through, and knotting together multiple, disparate strands of data, trying to construct a whole. In studying a faith community, patterns begin to emerge slowly—with patience, skill, and diligence—from the weaving of images, texts, artifacts, spaces, performances, conversations, narratives, histories, and observations (Goto, 2018: 86).

Goto also suggests that theologians studying a religious community need to think of it as "already wondrously knit together, a beautiful mystery with its own integrity and mind-boggling detail that the researcher has yet to grasp more fully" (Goto, 2018: 89). To answer the first part of the question at the head of this section then, when we talk about context in this book, we are using a combination of two of Goto's definitions: the background to, and the various circumstances of the gospel in the North of England; the whole social milieu, woven together, at this time and place in the North.

Like "context", culture is another word which different people use in different ways. Raymond Williams called it "one of the two or three most complicated words in the English language" (Williams, 2014: 87). The word is often used in the UK today to indicate something "posh" or "cultured". Elli did some research with church leaders in Hull in 2017,

culture

when it was the UK's City of Culture, and they often associated the word culture, on first thought, with things like fine art and classical music. This sense of culture as being associated with "high culture" originates in British thought in the nineteenth and early twentieth centuries, and the writings of Matthew Arnold, F. R. Leavis and T. S. Eliot. People also use the word "culture" to talk about the opposite of ballet and opera: a "popular culture" which is more down to earth, and might include football, pop music, bingo or boxing. There's also a third common understanding of culture: as people's experiences of life in a particular place and time. One of Elli's participants in Hull described this by saying "our culture is a part of us, it's a part of our character, our, the way we think, the way we view the world that we live in" (Wort, 2019: 56). This definition of culture is obviously very similar to Courtney Goto's description of context, as something that is woven together by "images, texts, artifacts, spaces, performances, conversations, narratives, histories, and observations" (Goto, 2018: 86). So, there's perhaps no wonder that theologians sometimes use those words interchangeably!

When we talk about culture in this book, we are following in the footsteps of the theologian Tim Gorringe. In *Furthering Humanity*, Gorringe described culture as the "name of the whole process in the course of which God does what it takes . . . to make and to keep human beings human" (Gorringe, 2004: 4). Under God, culture is the task of being human. It's everything that humans do or produce (individually or together), everything that arises from our behaviour and everything that drives us, including our worldviews, languages, accents; all the stuff of everyday life. And Gorringe sees the task coming from and coming out of this culture as nothing less than God's revolution:

> . . . the working out of the faith, hope and love of which Paul speaks: faith in the God who raised Jesus from the dead; hope in the possibilities for creation living under the God of hope; and arduous and patient work for a society which echoes or corresponds more closely to God's kingdom, which is the work of love (Gorringe, 2004: 265).

Mapping approaches to context

We've argued that context is a crucial component of theology: it shapes how we understand God through scripture, tradition, reason and experience, and is a method of understanding God in its own right. Contextual theology takes the idea of divine revelation seriously: that God reveals Godself throughout history and throughout the world in different ways.

But this leaves some people with a conundrum: does this mean that God is different in different contexts? If the gospel looks different in different contexts, which is the real gospel? Is there such a thing as *the* gospel? Isn't it more the case that there is one, true gospel message, which can be translated into different contexts? The latter position is the one that Bishop Steven Croft takes in his chapter in *Northern Gospel, Northern Church*. In this chapter, Bishop Steven argued that there is something distinctive about the North of England that gives it an identity that is not the same as other regions of England or parts of the UK, but that there is no gospel which is distinct to the North. Instead, he sees context as something Christians need to consider when sharing the gospel, to make sure we translate that core gospel message in the right ways in the right context. In a later chapter, Nigel offers a different perspective, arguing that it is the context which shapes the nature of the gospel in the North of England, and it is this thesis we are examining in the research in this book.

Steve Bevans, an American Roman Catholic missiologist, and one of the "fathers" of contextual theology, we might say (though he might try and deny that when face-to-face with us), helps us understand the different positions that people can take when doing contextual theology. In *Models of Contextual Theology* (2002), he describes six models of relating or combining context and gospel, which he describes as the translation, anthropological, praxis, synthetic, transcendental and countercultural models. We explain a bit more about each of them here (and it is also possible and instructive to overlay and compare them to Graham, Walton and Ward's seven methods of theological reflection).

The translation model, which is the one Bishop Steven Croft probably agrees with most, sees the message of the gospel as unchanging, faithful to an essential content. Christians in the pattern of this model try to find the kernel of the gospel and plant it into native ground. People engaged in this type of theology would look at their context for potential similarities to the gospel and communicate biblical ideas through these similarities. The context would be understood as not particularly good in and of itself, but as a place where the truth of the gospel can be planted (Bevans, 2002: 37–53). We sit more within Bevans' anthropological model. Instead of trying to translate the core message of the gospel into a context, the anthropological model examines that context closely, and looks for God and the gospel emerging from within it. The anthropological sees local contexts and different cultures as created by God, and therefore as places which teach us more about God (2002: 54–69).

With the praxis model, the gospel becomes an agent for change, like the South American liberation theologies we described earlier. This is a model where Christians are focused on action, and where theology is not seen as a finished product that is valid for all times and all places, but an understanding of and wrestling with God's presence in particular situations. Bevans identifies this model with liberation theology and its preference for the poor, as well as the discipline of practical theology, with its focus on a continuous cycle of action, reflection, action (2002: 70–87). In the countercultural model, Bevans argues some contexts are hostile to the gospel and need to be challenged by the gospel's liberating and healing power. With this model, the gospel represents an all-encompassing, radically alternate worldview that differs profoundly from human experiences of the world and the culture that humans create (2002: 117–137). Bevans gives the example of the Gospel and Our Culture Network in North America (inspired by Lesslie Newbigin's Gospel and Culture Network in the UK) which argued that the Church should always be a resident alien in the culture of the world (Bevans, 2002: 128).

Bevans describes Christians engaged in the synthetic model as trying to balance the insights of the translation, anthropological, praxis and countercultural models. This model preserves the importance of the gospel message and the heritage of traditional doctrinal formulations while at the same time acknowledging the vital role that context has played. This is a middle-of-the-road model, where every voice belongs at the theological table (2002: 89–102). Finally, there is the transcendental model, where Christians do their theologizing not by focusing on scripture, tradition or context, but by looking within. This model requires a change of mind, an awareness of the revelation of God within human experience, before any contextual theology can emerge (Bevans, 2002: 103–116).

Bevans also gives us a helpful map of how we might visualize these types. He describes a line with the anthropological model on the far left and the countercultural model on the far right (though Nigel disagrees about the positioning of the countercultural model!). Between these lie the praxis, synthetic, and translation models, with the transcendental model floating above "since it is more concerned with the theologizing subject than the theological content" (2002: 32). The models on the left take their understanding of God more from human experience and culture and put prominence on a theology of God's creation of the world. The models on the right take their understanding of God more from scripture and tradition and put prominence on a theology of God's redemption of the world.

We also wonder if these different ends of Bevans' map put different emphases on different persons of the Trinity. The countercultural and translation models put strong emphasis on understanding God through scripture and through the person of Jesus Christ. The anthropological model perhaps puts more emphasis on discerning God through the person of the Holy Spirit: the study of pneumatology. We mentioned above that contextual theology takes seriously the idea that God continues to reveal Godself throughout human history, that revelation was not a once-and-for-all event in the person of Jesus Christ. This theology understands the Holy Spirit to be at work actively in the world and wants to listen to where the Spirit is blowing. It is a theology which is open to listening to God, attentive to where God is working in the world, and to understanding how we might join in. This is the theology of the *missio Dei*. And we'll explain it further here and return to it again at the end of the book in Chapter 7.

Missio Dei

If you've not heard the term *missio Dei* before, you might take a guess that it's something about mission, and you'd be right. *Missio Dei* translates from Latin into English as "the mission of God". We often assume the Church has a mission to share the good news, and the idea of *missio Dei* shifts the focus. It's God who has a mission through history, to renew the whole of creation. God's out there getting on with the job, stirring up questions, calling people to faith and opening hearts, and it's our job to join in with God. In this idea, the Church doesn't have a mission, the mission has a Church (Bevans & Schroeder, 2011: 13).

Although the ideas, or better imagination, around the *missio Dei* are relatively new in the Church's tradition, it has long historical roots. Before the sixteenth century, the word "mission" was not used of the Church's task, but of relationships within the Trinity (Spencer, 2007: 9). "Mission" comes from the Latin "to send" and was used to describe how the Father "sends" the Son in the person of Jesus Christ, and how the Father and Son "send" the Spirit after Pentecost. From the sixteenth and seventeenth centuries onward, the word "mission" started to be used to refer to spreading of the faith: the Jesuits in Latin America started talking about "mission" as the human work of spreading the Christian faith (Spencer, 2007: 9). In the nineteenth century, the word began to be used more by Protestant churches, who commissioned missionaries: people who preached the gospel and called non-Christian people to conversion. This sense of the word "mission" was present in the naming of the Anglican "Church Missionary Society" in 1801 (Spencer, 2007: 10).

However, it was in the mid-twentieth century that the idea of the *missio Dei* started to be formed. In 1932, Karl Barth gave a talk where he described mission as an activity of God, something God and not the Church did, and the 1952 International Conference on Missions in Willingen, Germany, made explicit the link between God as Trinity and the mission of the Church: "The missionary movement of which we are a part has its source in the Triune God himself" (Bosch, 1991: 390). The Willingen conference made it clear that "the Church is a product of mission, rather than the other way round" (Spencer, 2007: 12).

Increasingly, *missio Dei* is becoming the main framework for understandings of mission across different church denominations. In his major evangelical study of the biblical roots of mission, Chris Wright uses the concept of *missio Dei* as a framework for his study. He argues we need to shift the focus in mission from human agency to God's purposes, from "missions" that we undertake to God's mission, and from a human/church perspective to God's perspective: "Mission is not ours; mission is God's" (Wright, 2006: 62). He argues that:

> In my view this is the key assumption of a missional hermeneutic of the Bible, i.e., the key that unlocks the whole flow of scripture . . . The more I have attempted to use . . . a missional map of the Bible, orientated fundamentally to the mission of God, the more it seems that not only do the major features of the landscape stand out clearly but also other less well-trodden paths and less scenic scholarly tourist attractions turn out to have surprising and fruitful connections with the main panorama (Wright, 2006: 64–9).

Missio Dei has also been the main Roman Catholic understanding of mission since Vatican II in the early 1960s. The report *Ad Gentes* (*To the People*) adopts a *missio Dei* stance: "The Church on earth is by its very nature missionary since, according to the Father, it has its origin in the mission of the Son and the Holy Spirit" (cited by Spencer, 2007: 13). *Missio Dei* is also a popular Anabaptist framework for mission (Kreider & Kreider, 2009). The Kreiders describe how, "at their best, Christian missionaries have always discovered that God is at work before they get there. And this is the task of all Christians who participate in God's mission: to expect to find God at work, and to be intensely alert to what God is doing" (Kreider & Kreider, 2009: 30). This is a great description of the *missio Dei*.

Earlier in this chapter, we mentioned Bevans and Schroeder's description of God as being like a dance, and how we can join in with God's dance throughout creation. They describe the dance of God, the movement of God, as this mission. They write that God doesn't *have* a mission, God *is* mission: "This is what God is in God's deepest self:

self-diffusive love, freely creating, redeeming, healing, challenging that creation" (Bevans & Schroeder, 2011: 10). They ask us:

> Do you want to dance? Do you want to join in that great Conga Line that has moved through the world since the beginning of time and that is also the heartbeat of God's deepest self? The dance will go on without us. It does not need us to continue its joyful progress among all peoples and in all times. But if we do join, we won't regret it. As we dance to bring wholeness and healing and peace in the world, we ourselves will become whole, be healed, and be graced with peace (Bevans & Schroeder, 2011: 17).

In this chapter, we have argued that God is calling to us out of our contexts and culture. God is already at work in our contexts, teaching us about who God is, and calling us to join in God's redemptive dance in that context. In the next chapter, we'll explore more about the context of the North of England and start to understand (in Courtney Goto's words) its own integrity and mind-boggling detail.

Questions for reflection

1. Where do you go to first to understand about God: scripture, tradition, reason or experience? Why do you think that is?
2. Can you think of ways that you might deepen your understanding of God by going to the sources that feel less familiar to you?
3. Can you think of ways that your context shapes how you understand God through scripture, tradition, reason or experience?
4. Which of Bevans' models of contextual theology felt most familiar to you? Why is that?
5. Can you think of a way your context has taught you something about God?

CHAPTER 2

The North and Northernness:
Defining context and culture

The North exists; it "is". The North is a "thing", a present reality. Very few people living in contemporary England, we imagine, would dispute these statements, whether it is "up here" or "up there" for them. And yet the North as a reality presents many conceptual difficulties and questions. Where does it begin and end? Who defines it, insiders or outsiders? If the North is a reality, what about Northernness—is that just as real or figment of the imagination? And if it is real what does it consist of? How come the North, and its associated Northernness, are so freighted with mostly negative connotations in national consciousness (if there be such a thing) and what might be done about that? And is its existence any help at all in addressing the often harsh realities it signifies? Where, if anywhere in the existence of the North and what comes with it in our imaginations, might there be good news, a gospel?

We touched on many of these questions in the earlier publication *Northern Gospel, Northern Church* (Wakefield & Rooms, 2016) and established some baselines that are repeated briefly here. At the same time, we'll be strengthening and developing our responses to such questions from a wider range of sources and literature in addition to data from the research we undertook.

Location and history

Where the North is, is a much more difficult question than it might at first seem. The Portico Prize for literature has been described as the "Booker of the North". It is named after the independent Portico Library in Manchester where I met Rachel Mann, one of its previous judges, for a discussion about it and the North in general, as background research for this book. In a further conversation with Thom Keep, the librarian, he described the relaunching of the prize in 2019 and a change in the criteria for submissions. He noted the insurmountable difficulty of deciding whether a particular book came "from the North" or was somehow located there. Writers from Yorkshire would ask if they were counted in! More seriously, applications also came from the borderlands between the North and the Midlands. A decision was made that the prize is now awarded (fascinatingly for our purposes) "for the book that best evokes the spirit of the North of England".[1]

It is worth noting that physical geology and geography play their part in the creation of the North. As Russell (2004: 22) points out, the vast majority of land over 2000ft in England is found from Derbyshire northwards. The northern, eastern and western borders of the North are fairly simple to note given the Scottish border and extensive coastlines. More problematical is where the southern boundary lies, as we saw above. Overall the nature of the land in the South and East of England and its associated weather patterns make it suitable for certain types of agricultural land use and settlement which are different to those to the North and West. Rivers too make significant barriers, at least in historical perspective. In my own view, the River Trent is an important marker of the N-S divide, though others work with the Mersey-Humber axis. For example, Russell distinguishes between the "far" and the "near" North and plumps for "seven counties" roughly north of the Humber-Mersey line (see his map, 2004: xii). All of our churches that we surveyed and researched were north of the Trent and the vast majority were in Russell's seven counties.

---

[1]   <https://www.theportico.org.uk/portico-prize-for-literature>, accessed 25 August 2020.

We noted in the previous work on the North (Wakefield & Rooms, 2016: 3–9) that human geographers, such as Danny Dorling, draw the N-S line in England between the Bristol Channel and the Wash since national inequalities, including life expectancy, are delineated on that axis. It roughly equates with the original "barrier" the Romans created in England against the North—the Fosse Way, which connected a series of defensive structures together (Jewell, 1994: 11) and runs from Exeter to Lincoln. In discussing the North, it is easy to overlook other regions such as the Midlands and the South-West. Nevertheless, as Russell notes (2014: 18), even on his tighter definition of the North, it is still the largest region in England, containing about one third of the land mass and population. As such it demands our attention over and above other regions.

As part of the preparation for this research I interviewed the historian, Michael Wood, who is perhaps best known for his televised storytelling of the history of England through archaeological work in one village in Leicestershire, Kibworth. Much of what he noted with me is underlined in historical depth by Helen Jewell's work (1994), and I summarize it very briefly here (for a longer reflection on the historical ebbs and flows of the power of the North see Gavin Wakefield's essay, pp. 55ff in *Northern Gospel*). In fact, it is worth beginning with Jewell's initial conclusion: "Analysis of the political, economic and social material indicates that the north-south divide is literally as old as the hills, *and has real manifestations throughout recorded history*" (1994: 6, my italics).

So, for more than a thousand years of its history, from Roman times the North was never subject to its southern neighbours, and it was therefore set apart. In an interesting aside, Michael Wood pointed out important migratory influences on the North over history on an East-West axis via, for instance, the Vikings to the East and much later Irish immigration to the West. The Venerable Bede writing in the North East (Jewell, 1994: 208) begins to codify a difference between northern and southern power blocs (while never travelling to the South!) which continues throughout the medieval period. However, the country as a whole, when it unites as a national entity before and after the Norman invasion, is increasingly dominated by the South (1994: 210), and while there are exceptions, these generally prove the rule. Sometimes used as a buffer against the Scots even further north, the North becomes somewhat redundant with the Union in the seventeenth century. This seems significant to us right up to today, given strong evidence that the South would rather ignore the North, unless it really must engage, e.g. at election time or in times of crisis such as the recent COVID-19 epidemic. We suggest this is an aspect of what we are going to call "othering", which we will need to return to later. The North's resurgence from a low point begins in the Industrial Revolution, at least in economic terms, while the rather derogatory term "provincial" comes into use in relation to London (Russell, 2004: 25). The South's dominance in defining language and culture solidifies from the 1890s onwards, with some brief flickering of a renaissance for the North on occasion in the twentieth century (2004: 28). By the end of that century, full industrial decline is being realized and today's inequalities are confirmed in many and varied ways.

We could build up more and more evidence for the existence of the North from geography, history and sociology, but our interest here is in what all this actually means. And here, as we noted when we set out, things become even more slippery.

Northernness

In discussing Northernness several issues arise straight away. The first is around how we define culture (thankfully we know some more about this now from the previous chapter, though there are differences between context and culture). Culture is the place we presume we are in when moving from the reality of a geographical region to what that means for the values, behaviour and lived experience of the people who make up that region.

This question around culture is made even more complex since, as we'll see, a lot of what is said about Northernness is at best developed from its relationship with the South and at worst delineated and even proscribed by people from the South. Addressing that question will raise further issues around how to understand and what to do about the power imbalance between the two regions.

Social and cultural anthropologists who study human behaviour have obviously thought a lot about culture since it emerged as a unifying idea for a number of behavioural phenomena in the nineteenth century. Inevitably it has come under much critique in the last fifty or so years, especially in relation to what is known as "essentialism". This is the mistaken idea that any given entity has unchanging and fixed properties which are its real true essence. The anthropologist Matthew Engelke (2017: 54) therefore says, when thinking about culture, that it is "not bounded in place; not fixed in time; not neat and tidy". In relation to Northernness, we can see immediately that this critique fits, since the imagination and behaviours associated with it can travel far and wide, it has certainly changed somewhat over time, and it is mixed up messily with many other cultural influences. The North of England is also part of the global Western consumerist world, is related to national traits within Englishness and there are other important effects upon its people, not least around the intersectionality of gender, sexuality, race and class. For readers unfamiliar with this idea, intersectionality is the way in which people's identities or the "social categories" that are ascribed to them interact and cross over with each other with the effect of multiplying or reducing their privilege, discrimination or disadvantage.

It is important therefore at this juncture to point out that the North is not synonymous, in an essentialist way, with the white working-class male—even though research shows this is a common trope associated with it (Milestone, 2016). Kate Fox, who we'll return to later, interviewed the performance artist Lemn Sissay for some research and she relates the conversation (Fox, 2017: 77):

> He told me that he didn't fit the "white, male" narrative of Manchester and didn't look like the version of it usually sold to the rest of the country. He asked, "So what happens when a young black man comes to Manchester and makes his name in poetry across the country and across different parts of the world? He still doesn't fit with the Manchester narrative, you know? So ergo, he's a threat to it."

There is a black community in Liverpool that can trace its roots back at least ten generations to the eighteenth century.[2] Significant populations of people of South Asian origin are notable right across the North and African-Caribbean ex-miners are being celebrated in a community project from Nottingham northwards.[3] Sheffield-based not-for-profit group Our Mel seeks to explore "cultural identity, Black history and what it means to be a person of colour in Britain today" and is therefore interacting with what it means to be black and Northern.[4]

The question this raises is whether there is anything at all that we can then talk about which constitutes Northernness, since accusations of essentialism do seem to fly about amongst those who write about it. Indeed, we ourselves in setting out with, as we discovered, our rather naïve research question could be accused of the same thing, in which case through an "excellent failure" we will hopefully be able to learn a great deal. It might be worth laying out a few positions on this question that we have come across in the literature and then work out what a reasonable stance of our own might be.

Russell quotes Donald Horne from a 1969 publication, *God is an Englishman*, which is interesting since it might be the only time that the Christian religion is dealt with in relation to Northernness (in this case in Britain as a whole) in the literature that we have come across:

> In the *Northern Metaphor* Britain is pragmatic, empirical, calculating, Puritan, bourgeois, enterprising, adventurous, scientific, serious and believes in struggle . . . In the *Southern Metaphor* Britain is romantic, illogical, muddled, divinely lucky, Anglican, aristocratic, traditional, frivolous, and believes in order and tradition (Russell, 2004: 26, italics in the original).

Russell himself creates a three-column list (2004: 37) which recognizes the difference between cultural production about the North and the

---

[2] <https://www.blackhistorymonth.org.uk/article/section/real-stories/liverpool-black-community-early-years/>, accessed 6 November 2020.

[3] <https://www.blackcoalminers.com/>, accessed 6 November 2020.

[4] <https://ourmel.org.uk/>, accessed 6 November 2020.

South, describes the northern self-image and how Northerners imagine the South. We think this is a helpful approach, and we reproduce here some, not all, of his table, giving a round ten characteristics overall that can be compared across the three perspectives.

External (especially southern) images of the North	Northern self-image	Northern images of the South
Truculent / carrying chip on shoulder	Independent	Subservient
Rude / lacking social graces	Blunt / straight-talking	Evasive / duplicitous
Hardworking	Hardworking / physically tough	Effete / wasteful / absorbing efforts and energy of the rest of country
Over-competitive / ungentlemanly	Competitive	Dilettante / lacking spirit
Philistine / unpolished, albeit highly musical	Practical / productive	Snobbish / wasteful / superficial
Mean	Careful with money	Wasteful
Homely	Friendly/Hospitable	Unfriendly / unsociable
Parochial	Proud of roots and identity	Cosmopolitan / rootless
Working class	Meritocratic / egalitarian	Nepotistic / elitist
Humorous if crude	Humorous / witty	Quick-witted but overly fond of *double-entendre*

We have plenty of evidence for what is being described here from our research, and we now offer a few illustrative examples from interviews with public figures and the research focus groups in the seven churches we visited.

I think we might add honesty to line 2 after an anecdote from the
Bishop of Burnley, Philip North, whom I interviewed on the subject of
Northernness. He moved to that position from London and was allowed a
formal conversation with the two archdeacons in Blackburn Diocese. He
was shocked that they answered all his questions openly and honestly for
ninety minutes without a hint of the somewhat duplicitous dissemination
he had become used to "down South".

The importance of roots and identity is made clear in this quote from
a lay leader in church B:

> Do I feel as though I'm from here? No, I don't, and I never will,
> but that's because of me, that I'm from Sheffield, and I'll always
> be from Sheffield, and I may never live in Sheffield again, but
> that doesn't matter. But I see the [my] kids grow up here, and
> the kids want to call [location] home and know that [location]
> is home and know that they've got some roots here that give
> them, if you want, northern, small [County] town identity, that
> I think is important to them in a way. And we may never leave
> here. We might do, I don't know, but it's that sense of belonging
> and involvement . . .

On friendliness one lay leader in church A remarked about their new
southern neighbours:

> I mean, across the road from us, there was a couple moved in,
> they still are there, from Southampton, and when they first came,
> they were amazed that we said "Good morning!"

And another following on in the same conversation on the link between
place, hospitality and even the formation of community:

> I'm really proud to be a Northerner, and I think I identify
> with people, including in [location], possibly, it's ex-mining
> community, I'm from a mining community . . . God's chosen
> to put me here, and if he put me in Southampton, I'd be doing
> what I did in Southampton. So, we think, I think Northerners

particularly, think that we're more welcoming, we're more friendly, and folk from the South tend to reinforce that to us, "Ooh, we don't get offered a cup of tea, you know, down where I come from," kind of thing.

We didn't focus on humour or go looking for it in the research, but having recognized its place we realized it is there in subtle and not so subtle joshing and bantering between the participants in some of the focus groups. And we found ourselves laughing with the groups from time to time. All of which is hard to capture in a short quotation, but we'll say more on this in Chapter 4. However, as a researcher, I always have ears open and my recent favourite example of northern humour relates to the football team I support. It is a comment, as I remember it, from the *Amber Nectar* Hull City AFC blog (now closed down) sometime in the team's slide from Premiership glory in the late 2010s, "You could have run the Northern Powerhouse on the number of men in the West Stand [at the KCOM Stadium in Hull] shaking their heads at half-time."[5]

We might extend Russell's list slightly, perhaps from the practical and blunt/honest to being authentic as we can see in parts of this conversation we have extracted from the leaders in church G discussing its very clear ups and downs:

> **Resp 1:** Yes. It's not all fantastic because it is a mixture, isn't it?
> **Interviewer:** *Because it's life.*
> **Resp 1:** Yes, exactly, it's real.
> **Resp 2:** Well, I was going to say, that's the word, it's real and I think that makes a difference.
> **Resp 3:** A bit more nitty-gritty.
> **Resp 1:** But it's grounded-ness, isn't it? I don't know whether we're lucky because grounded-ness is easier in the North.

---

5   There is further appreciation of the subtle humour involved here when one realizes that the "West Stand" is the, relatively speaking, slightly more genteel, higher class seating area as compared to the East Stand—where the "singing" normally comes from.

So, this is all very well but other commentators, as we noted above, still think such a list as Russell's smacks of essentialism. Key proponent in this school is Karl Spracklen, who is careful to recognize Russell's contribution (Spracklen, 2016: 10), but ultimately claims that it fails. He claims this is because it reifies or unhelpfully sets in stone the North's own view of itself when, he believes, this has been constructed by the more powerful southern voice through "hegemony"—the control of another through the use of economic, social or military domination:

> There is a hegemonic performativity imposed on the north by people with cultural power in the south of England, people who control policy-making, industries and popular culture . . . The hegemonic centre contrives culture to keep the north of England as dark as colonial depictions of Africa, a dangerous and savage place filled with post-industrial victims (Spracklen, 2016: 13).

Therefore, he claims Northernness is essentially a "made up" thing constructed from "various myths and invented traditions"—it is a *simulacrum,* something which has no origin or truth behind it at all. Following the postmodern sociologist and thinker Baudrillard he states, "The north has no essential existence in this framework because all we can ever know and share are the myths and narratives that allow us to construct and reproduce the simulacrum" (2016: 10).

One of the core characteristics of postmodernity that readers may be familiar with is that it disallows any "metanarrative" or overarching story with which to make sense of any particular phenomenon. Yet even for Spracklen there still has to be some framework to make sense of the paradox of the reality of Northernness (he eloquently describes his personal participation in it through beer with a proper head, Rugby League and the landscape itself) and the claim that it has no truth behind it. For this Spracklen turns to an understanding of magic and superstition (closely allied in his mind to religion and a form of Paganism):

> Northernness is a form of sympathetic magic, which northerners choose to perform, albeit through the constraints of hegemonic

cultural formations and the symbolic boundaries and invented traditions of imagined community (2016: 14).

And he makes therefore this, in our view, rather sad conclusion, since it cannot result in any transformative action:

> But we have no choice. We know we must continue to perform because without the performance of northernness, the north of England, the simulation and the imagined community, will collapse. Our northernness is our equivalent of the pagan cycle of the seasons. If we do not perform the rituals of the north, the sun will not rise tomorrow. So we go about our daily business of being northern (2016: 14).

It is possible, we believe, to hold a view in between the essentialist and the evacuated simulacrum. We first turn to Kate Fox, a "stand-up performance artist" who includes poetry and comedy in her work. She completed a PhD on her professional practice (Fox, 2017) reflecting on her experience as a northern, working-class woman making a living from all aspects of live performance.

Certainly, from solid evidence in her in-depth research interviews with northern performance artists, Fox agrees with both Russell and Spracklen with regard to how the "Northernness effect", as she terms it, is created via " . . . a classed and gendered cultural imperialism by which the [northern] region is stigmatized and Othered in relation to the more socially and economically powerful South of England" (2017: 55).

Using the concept of cultural capital (the capacity to inspire and be inspired),[6] which is not unrelated to spiritual capital, Fox describes how her research subjects experience a reduction in their cultural capital

---

[6] See a] p. 139 of Clive Marsh's book *A Cultural Theology of Salvation* (2018); he further discusses the various notions of spiritual, cultural, social and economic capital from pp. 135–142. And b] Bickley (2018), who builds his research in three North East communities around social capital (people), physical capital (buildings) and spiritual capital (purpose), hence the title of this Theos report.

simply by being northern. Both spiritual and cultural capital create social capital (relationality), which offers the possibility of increasing economic capital (money). Put simply northern performers find it more difficult to get people to their shows and make a career and a living. There are, however, negative and positive effects of this phenomenon:

> Its [Northernness] embodied elements—particularly accent and body size—automatically convert higher legitimate cultural capital into lower cultural capital and cause performers to be read as working-class, even though they might be read as middle-class on the basis of education and income. However, it potentially contains its own form of capital, which could be called Northern capital and is linked to values of *authenticity, community, humour and lack of pretension* (2017: 56, my italics).

It seems that Fox is onto something here beyond essentialism (while remaining critical of it—see 2017: 58–59) by noting the values embedded in northern capital. They are clearly connected with Russell's list but somehow lie deeper within the experience and meaning of Northernness and we will return to understanding them further at the end of the chapter. For now, I suggest such values are able to inform Fox's overall response to the "Northernness effect", which, as the title of her thesis suggests, is _resistance_. And at the same time, she sets that resistance within _affirmation_ of her public performing self, Northernness and her audience (2017: 109).

Perhaps an example might help here. Northerners when exposed nationally can easily fall into the essentialism of, what I can now name, "*Eddie Waring Syndrome*" (see also Russell, 2004: 260). If you were born after the early 1980s, you might not be aware of this northern sports commentator who popularized the game of Rugby League live on the BBC from the 1960s through to the end of the 1970s. His work was classically double-edged by the Northernness effect since on the one hand he, virtually single-handedly, popularized the sport in the national consciousness far beyond its northern heartlands, when every household now had a TV set. On the other hand, he did so by using and even exaggerating the very essentialist stereotypes of Northernness that we have been discussing. I can still hear him talking on my childhood TV about a player sent off for the "early bath", with the emphasis totally on the short vowel "a" in bath. We have faced the Eddie Waring syndrome too in this work on the North. The original book of essays we have referred to, *Northern Gospel, Northern Church*, was reviewed by Ian Bradley in *Modern Believing* (Bradley, 2017) in which he concluded that we had rather reinforced the grimness of the North over against debunking it. Thus, we need to place this current project within Fox's resistance to the essentializing of the North (especially around gender, class and colour, as we noted earlier), and our intuition to go looking for good news or gospel does seem to be the right one.

A theological point might support our position here. Christianity is a *theistic* religion and while, from an outsider's perspective, it may lend itself to accusations of magic, in its truest forms it is set firmly against such forms of religion. Some believers even decry naming Christianity as a religion at all. Theism is the belief that God's relationship with the world is one of constant upholding in every moment without separating God from the world (deism) or equating the world with God (pantheism). The incarnation of God, the Word in Jesus Christ as a human being, thickens our understanding of this relationship in a particular moment in time and space which becomes universally true (so Christians claim) in all time and space. Therefore culture, just like anything else in God's created world, is indwelt by God and redeemable for God's purposes. Our approach to culture then, theologically, following Max Warren, is to take off our shoes, for it is holy ground. This is not to essentialize it, but neither is it to treat it as a form of magic. Northernness, we believe, cannot be a "simulacrum" with no contribution to make to God's promises and purposes for the world.

Clive Marsh in his book *A Cultural Theology of Salvation* (2018) undertakes the task of looking for the meaning of salvation through historical and contemporary cultural artefacts, and in doing so he updates Paul Tillich's theological method to help him. We had better not go into too much detail here, but our task is to do a very similar thing with Northernness to that which Marsh does with, say, the USA TV series *Breaking Bad* and *The Big Bang Theory*; discover what Paul Tillich called the *Gehalt* or "depth-content" within it and how that connects with the kingdom of God and the gospel of salvation. This requires us not to be simply *extracting* meaning (Marsh, 2018: 40) in the essentializing manner we have seen happening, but rather to take off our shoes, listen carefully and critically and discern the God-givenness of Northernness. This, in Marsh's terms, is to ask (2018: 42), "How does what is being interpreted [in our case Northernness] help us better discern and fashion human action in anticipating the kingdom of God which is yet to be?" The kingdom, Marsh points out, has a future orientation which we could add inevitably leads to action. This is what is missing in magic, which only leaves us with more of the same.

We have therefore positioned this work, we hope, between essentialism and the simulacrum. What remains is to offer potential responses to the "othering" of the North and to name that as a slightly less full-blown version of colonialism we are going to call *coloniality*. In doing so, we will give content to and draw from Fox's affirming and resistant position. We'll then be able to offer a sense of the good news inherent in Northernness, which will inform the rest of the book.

Othering and coloniality

We have seen strong evidence of the othering of the North by the more powerful South. This must not be read as more "chip on the shoulder" from Northerners (see Russell's table above and Croft's comment in Wakefield and Rooms, *Northern Gospel*, 2016: 32). The Northernness effect is real, and it hurts the identity and the pockets of many people including cultural producers such as comedians. Neither is it some well thought out strategy consciously conducted by millions of people. Like ageism, sexism and many other isms it is a way of treating other people as alien, different and therefore incommensurate with what is proper, right and normal.

We suggest that, following an examination of the metaphor of "up" (see Wakefield and Rooms, 2016: 224) in the way that the North is always up in relation to the rest of the country, this isn't just because of the way maps are oriented. The North is up because it is unknown (cf. the saying, "it's all up in the air") and therefore to be feared, even perhaps hated sometimes.

Robert Heaney, in his book which aims at "Finding God and each other amidst the hate" (2019), describes such othering, when embedded in long historical imbalances of power which aren't overt, legally driven colonialism, as *coloniality*. And coloniality isn't just more complaint or "chippiness", it is "a category that connects experiences of subjugation and resistance across a range of historical settings" (2019: 69). Heaney gives voice to what might be done through resistance about coloniality or what we might call northern othering. Just as Marsh above, he calls for a "deeper critical awareness" (2019: 76), thus making those made invisible by their othering visible or, to put it another way, the unknown known. Since this and the previous volume of essays are the first overtly theological books to address the subject of the North in breadth and depth, we'd like to think that this project is part of that resistance, of making the North known. God also needs to be made visible within the conditions of coloniality, "amidst the hate" (2019: 78), as it were, which takes us again to the task of this book. Heaney offers the two-fold task of resistance therefore as turning away from the *status quo* (2019: 81) and turning towards the "colonized Christ who makes the invisible visible" (2019: 84) because he lived and died under the yoke of Empire while challenging and subverting it. We'll return to discuss more of Heaney's book in Chapter 6. For now, we note that there is plenty of evidence in our interviews with new or fairly new northern Christians that they are made visible by Christ, not least when discussing the Eucharist as below from church D:

> **Resp 1:** How I vision [it—the Eucharist] is that there's wires coming from upstairs straight down to all different people all over the world and everybody's got their own wire connected to Jesus and especially so on Sundays. When you go and do your communion part, you say your little prayer and that's your connection time.
>
> **Resp 2:** His body and blood are together . . . It's the closest you get to him [Jesus] because it's [the bread and wine] a part of him. [Silence]

Thus, we might discern here a need, which I uncovered some years ago when first studying the relationship between faith and culture, for what we could call a creative relationship in the tension between "affirmation and resistance". These are the two words we noted above that Kate Fox uses (2017: 109) for her response to the intersectional experience of subjugation as a northern, working-class woman, but they correlate closely, I would suggest, with Andrew Walls' indigenizing and pilgrim principles developed from his work (1996) that we referred to in the previous chapter. Indigenizing takes the particularity of culture and context utterly seriously in affirmation, while the pilgrim principle refuses to be naïve about any culture, but accepts there is a pilgrimage journey of transformation and liberation to go on which discerns and resists the dark and dysfunctional aspects of it.

Affirmation and resistance

Returning to the idea of a deep *Gehalt* in Northernness, beyond Russell's potentially essentializing list, Fox's unearthing of the northern values of authenticity, community, humour and lack of pretension is "gold dust" in this research. I believe we can confirm these values and use them as fuel for resistance to coloniality as experienced in the North. They become the basis for discerning and even announcing the good news of the kingdom. If we conflate lack of pretension with authenticity, since it is probably an effect of it, then we have discerned three values embedded in Northernness which we name as the gifts of this context and culture to the kingdom and the mission of God in the world.

Authenticity
Authenticity is an ideology ubiquitous in contemporary Western societies according to anthropologists (Engelke, 2017: 201) so it is perhaps no surprise that we come across it here and that Chris Baker in a recent article makes important connections for the value of authenticity in mission in the postmodern and postsecular world (Baker, 2017). It is worth noting too that authenticity has come under serious critique from philosopher Charles Taylor (2018 [1991]), at least in its more extreme

individualistic and even narcissistic forms. Nevertheless, there is value in being true to oneself, if that self is understood as being formed in community—the second of our northern values.

Two examples of resistance to othering from Fox's work might be helpful to illustrate how affirming authenticity in Northernness can be turned to liberative effect. Fox suggests that if we consciously and authentically "come out" as northern that allows the possibility of "re-signifying" the labels that are thrust upon us from the outside (2017: 101) thus changing the nature of the othering discourse "from within" (2017: 105). This is the same move the gay community made in adopting the initially pejorative term "queer" for themselves such that it changed its meaning altogether and became a cause for joy and celebration amongst the community.

Second, and perhaps an extension of re-signifying, is what Fox calls "talking back" (2017: 104). If we are authentic, true to ourselves, our culture and our context, then it is possible to call out what the other sees in us and projects onto us in their othering. To name it for what it is, to hold it up for examination and scrutiny. Once again this is not to retreat into chippiness but is an assertive move which reaches towards inclusivity and equality. And without the second value of community such a move can easily slip into a deepening rather than a healing of the gulf between us and the other.

Community

We noted clearly in our focus group data earlier in the chapter the importance of community as friendship and hospitality, at the very least to our respondents. Authenticity makes the best sense when arising from community and we suggest, again following Fox, allows for the possibility of inhabiting the space between ourselves and the other differently. Fox notices the liminal, or "betwixt and between", trickster nature of her public performances and, by paying attention to that space between, realizes that a new kind of performer-audience relationship can emerge. One which is characterized by a decision she notes, on the part of one of her interviewees, to "love the audience" (2017: 103).

It was Martin Luther King Jr. who said, in effect, that those you wish to change you must first love (2010 [1963]). This is not in any sense romantic love, but a public loving which builds on respect and esteem, wills the best for the other despite their potential and sometimes very real antagonism. Perhaps it is indeed love that knocks the chip from our northern shoulders that we might engage out of our commitment to community, hospitality and friendship.

It is not a very big step, in my view, when discussing a commitment to community, to find its source in the Christian God, the One who is community in Godself, the three-in-one. Where community is forming, where love does love's work in public, there God is.

Humour

Humour is a theme we have unearthed in this research in the writing of this chapter and not just because we have been interacting with the work of a northern stand-up comic and poet. It is true though that any research journey is continuous and reflecting on this new idea to us has been a surprise as well as a welcome addition to our findings. We think it is worth extending the idea of humour a little here.

Steven Croft notes in the essay we have referred to several times (Wakefield & Rooms, 2016: 22) two possibilities when "telling the story" of the North, which he draws from James Hopewell's classic study of the narrative congregations tell about themselves (1988). They are the romantic and the tragic telling, and Croft thinks there is an unhelpful emphasis on the tragic told by and about the North. We have seen how this plays out in othering and coloniality.

However, Hopewell offered two other types or genres of story to add to the romantic and the tragic—they are the comic and the ironic (1988: 58, 61). While bigger than just humour, since comic stories turn out well and integrate difference, and ironic stories deny the possibility of heroes and deal with the dreadful realities of life (perhaps pointing once again to authenticity), nevertheless we would be foolish to miss the connections here to the possibilities of "telling the North" in such a way as to resist othering. It might also be fun since both genres generally produce a laugh or two along the way.

I have written elsewhere about the importance of irony within the Christian story itself (Rooms, 2012: 91) following William Lynch, who was sure that faith without irony can lead to fury (Lynch, 1973: 102) (and perhaps we might add even hate, according to Heaney). So once again we connect the *Gehalt* of Northernness to the gospel, which is most often upside-down where the last come first. Another example from Hull is apposite. While Elli researched attitudes to Hull as City of Culture in 2017, I continued my support in the away end at an occasional Tigers match. Resistance and irony were in abundance in the chant: "We know who we are, we know who we are, we're City of Culture, we know who we are."

Questions for reflection

1. How do the ideas of essentialism (the "fixing" of culture in a freeze-frame), coloniality (subjugation of the other, though not as overt as in colonialism itself) and *Gehalt* (the deep content, meaning and values embedded within a culture and its cultural practices) sit with you? If they are new ideas how might they expand your thinking, even your horizons? Where might you go to understand more about them?

2. How would you compare and contrast what we have attempted in this chapter with the previous one? Have we been faithful to the methods and approaches to contextual theology set out there?

3. If you consider yourself a northerner—how aware are you of both your cultural capital and the dangers of what we termed "*Eddie Waring Syndrome*"? How might affirmation and resistance work out for you in your current location?

4. What is it about Christians and humour? We recognized we missed it as a theme in our research, and we needed others outside the faith to lead us to it. How might we bring comedy, irony and laughter more to the front and centre of how we believe and act?

CHAPTER 3

After Christendom: It's the end of the world as we know it

In the last two chapters, we explored how studying our context and culture allows us to understand more about God and what the specific context and culture of the North teaches us about the concept of Northernness and its relationship to the gospel. But before we dig more deeply into the details of what God is doing in our northern churches today from our research, it will help us to explore further the wider context in which they exist. That exploration will address how the relationship of Church and world has changed in recent times in our nation, "after Christendom".

The subtitle for this chapter is a song by the American band REM from 1987. Fans of REM will of course know that our chapter title isn't the full title of the song; the song is called "*It's the end of the world as we know it (and I feel fine)*". Michael Stipe's lyrics are (as always) relevant. The world that we know, the Church that we know, may be coming to a finale, but it's ok. As Christians we know that the death of the old is nothing to be feared, that new life can always spring from a seemingly hopeless situation, and that an empty tomb follows the cross. These are the themes we explore in detail in this chapter.

The world in which the Church exists in the UK is dramatically different from how it was fifty years ago. A good example of this rapid change is the BBC police procedural series *Life on Mars* where our detective hero has an accident in 2006 and wakes up in 1973. He is faced with a police force which is essentially "on another planet" with attitudes and behaviours that are unrecognizable from even just thirty-three years ahead. And think of the changes that have occurred especially in the digital world since 2006.

Even if you've never thought critically about this, if you're a certain age you'll have recognized it in your gut. If you were born in the 1940s or 1950s, you may remember churches being much fuller when you were a child. You may remember every pew being filled at Easter and Christmas. You were probably taught a lot of Bible stories at school. You may be surprised that your grandchildren don't know the stories and hymns you knew as a child. Moreover, you may feel that the Church is taken a lot less seriously than it used to be. You may feel in your heart that the Church used to be a lot more important than it is now. You may even feel that, as a Christian, you're in exile in your own country.

In the churches that we visited across the North of England, we saw this sense of exile in several ways. Many of our churches described recent histories of the church feeling divorced from the communities they served. There had been no church in our research location D for three years and virtually all the others that had members in the locality had closed sometime before that. The church was truly dead in that place. Research church C had to create a new worshipping community for its congregation of homeless people and people experiencing addiction, as the local churches seemingly couldn't cope with them. Churches B and E had substantial reordering in the 1980s and 2000s, as the traditional church buildings were not serving their community's needs; church A was planning a complete reordering. Similarly, one of the churches in location G had been converted from a parish church to a chapel of ease as the parish could not afford to keep the traditional model of church going. In the benefice of F, five different parish churches had to be grouped together under one incumbent, and relationships had broken down between the churches, which were used to being independent. This story of relationships breaking down under the pressures of the post-Christendom world was also experienced by church D, when apparently, as we were told, the outgoing churchwarden threw the church keys at the archdeacon on the final day, as the church door was locked for the last time.

Christendom

One way of describing this shift for the Church in this country is to explore how the UK has moved from being in what is known as a Christendom context to a post-Christendom context. Christendom refers to the period of time when Christianity was a major part of the local culture, was the official religion of a country, or a significant political power. In Christendom, the Church participates in, or is allied with, the dominant forms of social, cultural, economic and intellectual life (Brueggemann, 1997: 38). There are lots of ways the "settlement" between Church and State is worked out and in England this is sometimes called "weak Establishment" since, unlike historically in some Scandinavian countries (and even currently in Denmark), the Government does not employ Church clergy and organists as a special type of religious "civil servant".

In the decades after Jesus' death and resurrection, the Church certainly wasn't in a Christendom culture. The early Christians were often persecuted: tortured, imprisoned and killed for their faith by the Roman Empire. The Christian faith, with its radical insistence that there was only one God—Father, Son and Holy Spirit—demanded its followers' total allegiance. It is worth staying with this pre-Christendom world for a moment as it might connect in several ways with the post-Christendom world we now experience.

The Epistle from Mathetes to Diognetus from the second century CE says these intriguing things about Christians from a writer outside of the faith, but observing them sympathetically:[7]

> For Christians are not distinguished from the rest of mankind
> either in locality or in speech or in customs. For they dwell not
> somewhere in cities of their own, neither do they use some
> different language, nor practise an extraordinary kind of life.
> Nor again do they possess any invention discovered by any
> intelligence or study of ingenious men [sic], nor are they masters

---

7   For the full Epistle see <http://www.earlychristianwritings.com/text/diognetus-lightfoot.html>, accessed 10 March 2020.

of any human dogma as some are. But while they dwell in cities of Greeks and barbarians as the lot of each is cast, and follow the native customs in dress and food and the other arrangements of life, yet the constitution of their own citizenship, which they set forth, is marvellous, and confessedly contradicts expectation. They dwell in their own countries, but only as sojourners; they bear their share in all things as citizens, and they endure all hardships as strangers. Every foreign country is a fatherland to them, and every fatherland is foreign. They marry like all other men [sic] and they beget children; but they do not cast away their offspring. They have their meals in common, but not their wives. They find themselves in the flesh, and yet they live not after the flesh. Their existence is on earth, but their citizenship is in heaven. They obey the established laws, and they surpass the laws in their own lives. They love all men [sic], and they are persecuted by all. They are ignored, and yet they are condemned. They are put to death, and yet they are endued with life. They are in beggary, and yet they make many rich. They are in want of all things, and yet they abound in all things. They are dishonoured, and yet they are glorified in their dishonour. They are evil spoken of, and yet they are vindicated. They are reviled, and they bless; they are insulted, and they respect. Doing good they are punished as evil-doers; being punished they rejoice, as if they were thereby quickened by life.

It seems the early Christians took their context absolutely seriously, but were not fixed in it or enthralled by it. Yet as that early Christian church grew, more and more Romans became converts to the faith. Some of these Romans were people in positions of power and influence, which in turn influenced more of their fellow officials.

The great shift for Christianity, from being a persecuted and marginalized religion to being allied with power, came in the year 312 when the Emperor Constantine converted to Christianity. Visitors to York Minster will have seen his imposing statue at the south side of the cathedral: Constantine was in York when he was appointed Emperor of Rome, and so the North played its own part in this story. Constantine knew about Christianity from his mother, the Empress Helena, who is remembered as St Helen by some churches. The legend goes that before the Battle of the Milvian Bridge, when Constantine fought against the rival Emperor Maxentius, he saw a vision of a cross in the sky, and writing saying, "By this sign conquer" (Eusebius, 1945: 27). He took this to mean that the Christian God would give him victory over his rival, and his subsequent victory confirmed the power of God in his mind. Constantine eventually converted to Christianity, and the Christian faith became the official religion of the Roman Empire.

Since that point, Christianity has been allied with power in Western Europe. Of course, the idea of Christendom, where the Church is in a position of power, does not hold true for most of the world over these centuries: Christianity was, and often still is, a minority religion in many countries and continents. The persecution of Christians in certain countries today shows us that the idea of Christendom is not universally applicable. But in the UK, the Church has been allied to government and power for centuries.

One good example of this will be familiar to those of you who did Tudor history at school. When the pope refused to give Henry VIII a divorce from Catherine of Aragon, he declared that the English Church should be separated from the Roman Catholic Church. From that point in 1533 the monarch has been Head of the Church of England, and Elizabeth II still has the title of "Defender of the Faith". But the link between political power and the Church in the UK has not always been static and simple. That link has been negotiated and renegotiated at many periods in our country's history, such as during the Civil War and the Commonwealth. And the link between political power and the Church has not always meant that all the people of the UK were Christian, or even went to church. This was the situation that John Wesley faced in the eighteenth century.

Wesley lived at a time when there were huge changes in people's lives in Britain. The UK had been very much a rural country, but as the Industrial Revolution drew people to better paid jobs in factories, hundreds of thousands of people moved into the cities and towns. And as people moved to the cities, they often stopped attending church: partly because they were dislocated from their traditional way of life, and partly because these growing cities often had no churches. It took a lengthy Act of Parliament to create a new parish, so there were often no churches at all in new industrial areas (Davies, 1963: 31). At this point, more than 90 per cent of the population officially belonged to the Church of England (Rack, 2002: 10). But the numbers of people actually going to church were very low, with only 5 per cent of the population attending church and receiving communion: much more like the numbers today (Hylson-Smith, 1997: 82). And it seems as though the Church of England was quite happy with this situation: we can imagine the clergy of Jane Austen's novels going into the Church as a career move from educated and aristocratic backgrounds. They were the product of Christendom: if only people from privileged and powerful backgrounds can become leaders in the Church, that Church will be made in the shape of privilege and power. These clergy had little in common with factory workers living in slum housing, and there were few churches in industrial areas. The new urban working class were forgotten by the official Church, and priests like Wesley who felt called to minister to these communities and people were few and far between.

You may feel that the picture that Wesley faced in the eighteenth century has a lot of parallels with the Church in today's world: a population forgotten by its national Church, and a church culture on the ground at odds with the majority of the population. But there are a lot of differences too: our clergy aren't sipping sherry in the drawing rooms of the landed gentry nowadays, and our churches *do* want to engage with the people around them. So why does it still feel as though the Church is in exile?

Post-Christendom

We described above how Christendom is a context in which the Church has, or is allied to, the political and governing power in a country. We saw that one of the risks of a Christendom Church is that it can become distanced from the majority of people in a country. And this is one of two main features of post-Christendom; the Church is distanced from the population *and* has lost most of its political and societal power. The British Anabaptist theologian Stuart Murray Williams describes post-Christendom having two main features: the story of Christianity is unknown, and the Church is alien to life in the UK (Williams, 2004: 3).

But how did the Church in the UK get to this point? In his book *Post-Christendom: Church and Mission in a Strange New World*, Williams gives six main reasons for the slow decline of Christendom in Western Europe over the centuries:

1. Disillusionment with religion resulting from incessant warfare between supposedly Christian nations.
2. The increasing reliance of philosophers and scientists on reason and scientific experimentation rather than revelation in the Enlightenment period.
3. The impact of industrialization and urbanization on traditional beliefs and structures.
4. The influence of postmodernism.
5. The persistence of dissent and emergence of the "free church" tradition.
6. The globalization of the Church and its mission (Williams, 2004: 179).

Williams argues that the urbanization and industrialization described above, and the institutional Church's lack of response, eventually led to many people rejecting the Church of England. This was even more sharply evident amongst the working class. The Methodist Church had some success here but even there, a process of "gentrification" was observable over time. He shows how many people were left unimpressed by the Church's response to the arguments of Enlightenment philosophers in the eighteenth century, and proponents of postmodernism in the late twentieth century. He describes the effect of World Wars One and Two, where each side claimed they were on the side of God, but the horrors of the trenches, the Holocaust and the Gulag left many people without faith in a God who could allow these atrocities to happen.

This shift is something that Lesslie Newbigin also described in his important little book *Proper Confidence* (1995). Newbigin links the individualism and certainty of Descartes' dictum "I think, therefore I am", which drove the project of scientific reason throughout the

Enlightenment, in a straight line to Nietzsche's "will to power" (1995: 26). He shows how all truth can now be manipulated by the powerful (an effect we continue to see in the populism of our own day). Newbigin argued that with the Enlightenment's eradication of doubt, knowledge is equated with "scientific" certainty, and the Soviets could pursue power through science (1995: 45), and by extension, we could argue, on the other side of the twentieth-century ideological divide, the Nazis could attempt the extermination of whole people groups in mass technological death.

Finally, Williams describes how the emergence of the "free churches" (i.e. those churches not part of the Anglican or Roman Catholic denominations) and the globalization of mission ironically added to the end of Christendom by positing faith as more personal and private than public (believing not belonging). In fact, the individualizing and privatizing of Christian faith affected all churches eventually such that now there is evidence in UK churches that in general they rarely act in public as a Christian body of believers.

In globalization, we can also trace a link between the de-industrialization of the North of England and the end of Christendom. Just as the Church failed to respond adequately to massive industrialization in the eighteenth and nineteenth centuries, when globalization struck these industries in the twentieth the Church seemed even more powerless in the face of such worldwide effects. A vicious circle appears since what is happening in the community is always present in voluntary institutions within that community. When jobs are lost and money is tight, the local church has tended to turn inward rather than outward, which only hastens its death.

So, the Christian Church is left high and dry in the UK with an unknown story and an alien institution. George Lings has described the move from Christendom to post-Christendom as like a local church moving from being in a valley to the top of a hill. In Christendom, the Church lies at the bottom of a metaphorical "cultural valley", and people are naturally rolled into it by the gravity of the way the culture operates. The culture expects and knows they will be there as there is a "plausibility structure" existing in society for Christian belief. In post-Christendom, the Church is up on top of a hill: it can sing praise songs as loudly as it likes, celebrate the liturgy as meaningfully as possible, but the cultural gravity is working all the time against it. People will not naturally gravitate to the Church since belief in the God who is born as a human being, lives, dies and is resurrected to live for ever is thought of in society as untenable and even somewhat shameful. The answer to this problem, fairly obviously, is that the Church has to come down from the top of the hill to be with the people (and as we'll argue from the research throughout the rest of this book).

At this point, it might be worth offering a slightly different "valley analogy" for those readers who could object that in their context Christendom still operates to some extent—people still bring their bairns for christening; the church coffers in the village are full because people value its presence amongst them. Setting aside what actually happens when a christening family and the traditional congregation actually meet in the same worship event or what the closing of a village church might do to local house prices, we acknowledge that the vestiges of Christendom are still present in some places. Yet we claim the sun that shone in Christendom is setting over the western horizon. Some churches still receive the last rays of the setting sun. But others are in complete shadow where it is virtually night already. We wonder whether there are more places where the sun of Christendom has set in the North of England—certainly the evidence cited above would point to this. And even in the places where there is still some light, the sun is still inexorably setting. What is true now for those churches in the dark shadow will be true for the others still enjoying the last rays of sunshine in a few years' time. This places churches, where already "something is happening" in the twilight of Christendom (such as our research communities), *at the forefront of the future of the Church.* We can't underestimate the importance of this conclusion from our research for the future of UK churches—paying attention to these living, breathing, somewhat vibrant, if fragile churches in the North offers us blueprints for what is possible and sustainable across the whole country—North, South, East and West. Thus these northern churches and what is happening in them can be a gift to the country as a whole. We'll come back to this point and underline it further in Chapter 6.

It may feel all very well to discuss terms like Christendom and post-Christendom, and the historical causes of both, but what does that actually mean to those of us alive and working in the Church today? For some of us, it may feel like being in exile in our own country.

Exile

This idea of the Church being in exile in today's culture is not new and has been explored extensively over many years by the American Protestant theologian Walter Brueggemann. Brueggemann compares the place of the Church in contemporary Western culture to the Jews in exile in the Old Testament. Although he is writing about the Church in the USA, Brueggemann's description of a Church which experiences the loss of a "structured reliable 'world' where . . . treasured symbols of meaning are mocked and dismissed" may feel familiar to many in the UK (Brueggemann, 1997: 3). Some similarities that Brueggemann finds between the Church today and Israel in exile are that "the community of faith had to live in a context where it exercised little influence over public policy", "the temptations to cultural syncretism and the disappearance of a distinct identity were acute", and that "in the face of political irrelevance and social syncretism, a main task of the community was to work very hard and intentionally at the . . . development of strategies and mechanisms for survival" (Brueggemann, 1997: 104–105).

In a later work (2014), Brueggemann offers a three-fold way through exile encapsulated in his book's title: *Reality, Grief, Hope*. Reality about admitting the situation we are in (where church doors are closing for the last time); grief and therefore lament for what we have lost in Christendom, which nevertheless allows us to thank God for it, let it go and move on. The third strategy and mechanism for survival is "the intense practice of hope" (see also Brueggemann, 1997: 106). This is a theme that has been picked up by other authors, who argue that the Church should be rejoicing in the exile we find ourselves in. Australian theologian Michael Frost writes that:

> We have been building churches for an era that has slipped out from under us. The Christendom era has fallen. Now church leaders find themselves cut off and alone in an increasingly

foreign culture that is antagonistic to them . . . However, there
are other voices that express real hope—not in the reconstruction
of Christendom, but in the idea that the end of this epoch
actually spells the beginning of a new flowering of Christianity.
The death of Christendom removes the final props that have
supported the culturally respectable, mainstream, suburban
version of Christianity . . . I, for one, am happy to see the end of
Christendom. I'm glad that we can no longer rely on temporal,
cultural supports to reinforce our message or the validity of our
presence. I suspect that the increasing marginalization of the
Christian movement in the West is the very thing that will wake
us up to the marvellously exciting, dangerous and confronting
message of Jesus (Frost, 2006: 4–9).

Patrick Whitworth, a theologian, church planter and priest in the Church
of England, picks up Brueggemann's metaphor of a Church in exile, and
gives six principles that an exiled Church should follow:

Incarnational mission: "For Jesus, mission involved complete
commitment and utter vulnerability to those to whom he had
come. Likewise, the church today can no longer come on its own
terms, as it did in the days of Christendom, to the population at
large, but rather it must come with humility . . . " (Whitworth,
2008: 113).

Contextual mission: "If a church persists in keeping a model of
church that is far removed from the culture of its host community
. . . then it will simply fail to communicate with the people in
those cultures and so fail in its missionary objective. In that case
it will have retreated into a kind of self-imposed exile rather than
being an exilic community seeking to draw into its fellowship
those who are attracted by its message and life" (2008: 115–16).

Radical mission: "Is there not a call to a radical return to our
own vocation, living in the context as we do of other empires? . . .
To be radical is to return to our most basic calling, to rediscover
the root of our faith, to focus on Jesus in a way fitting for our
times . . . The second way in which we are called to be radical is

to simply present Jesus (rather than Christianity) in a way which invites participation rather than confrontation" (2008: 120).

Spiritual mission: "An authentic spiritual life" which resonates throughout the entirety of Christian life at home and at work as much as in church, and not "a show for specifically religious occasions" (2008: 123).

Communal mission: "A vital part of Jesus' ministry was the formation of a new community" (2008: 125).

Relational mission: "There is a widespread desire in our broken lives of twenty-first-century Britain for stable, meaningful, close relationships" (2008: 127).

So, Whitworth leaves us with a challenge. Do we withdraw into a self-imposed exile, continuing to be irrelevant to the communities and people around us, or do we embrace being on the margins? There is great potential in marginality: if we embrace being a marginal Church, can we join in with the others on the margins of society, those whom Jesus came to serve? We'll spend some initial time now explaining how our research churches have begun to make this move, and we'll delve much more deeply into what we discovered they are doing in the next chapter.

Northern churches in exile

We described at the beginning of this chapter how closed churches were one of the signs of a post-Christendom culture in the northern churches we visited for this research. However, for the churches we visited, where we had been told that "something was happening", we found they had embraced that exile as Whitworth recommends above, with incarnational, contextual, radical, spiritual, communal and relational mission and ministry.

We saw one example of the incarnational mission that Whitworth recommends in church G. This was the area where one of the churches had been relegated from a parish church to a chapel of ease in 2009. Despite the fact there was no longer a viable worshipping community in this building, the local group of churches did not abandon the people in this area of their community. It was a patch which had once seen people working in the shipyards: visiting this area, you could see where the shipyard had once stood, now a derelict patch of land. The houses in this part of town were once-serviceable terraces and were now houses of multiple occupancy with boarded-up windows and damaged doors. But the church kept serving the people of the area, turning the church building into a community centre. They now hold a coffee and craft morning, a healthy eating club, digital drop-ins, line dancing and much, much more. They partner with other groups who run Brownies and Guides, a Credit Union, and a playgroup for little children. The church had remained present in these streets, humbly serving the community, and not demanding attendance on their own terms. One of the groups that meets in the building is a morning drop-in for older people, who have a cuppa and stay for a soup lunch. The church had started this group to tackle loneliness in the community, but found it became more than that: the people attending the morning drop-in asked if they could have a communion service before their soup lunch. For these people, the building was still a church, not a community centre. It was their church, and they wanted to meet with God there.

Whitworth describes contextual mission as close engagement with the community, and we clearly see this in the example above. We also saw this at church B. This church is in a historic town of 15,000 people, where a new estate of more than 1,000 homes is also being built. This is a town with two sides: a middle-class community who might meet in the converted mill with micro-brewery and up-market delicatessen, and then communities of working-class and migrant people who occupy the terraced housing where the mill workers once lived. Although the church in the workers' part of town has received considerable investment from members who have found financial success, it is still closely engaged with the needs of the people in its community, running a foodbank, supporting Christians Against Poverty, and partnering with a project to help substance abusers and addicts through exercise. This church is in a financial position that might make other churches very envious, but its mission is still focused on transforming the lives of the people in the community it serves. They have not retreated into an exiled position, but as Whitworth urges, are engaging new people at their "edge" with a gospel message and life (Whitworth, 2008: 115–16). We'll unpack what that message consists of in the next two chapters.

We mentioned our research location D earlier, where the church building closed down in 2014 and the new church community had to originally meet in the vicar's house. This gives us one example of the radical and spiritual mission Whitworth describes, focused on the person of Jesus and with an authentic spiritual life. The Eucharist is central to the church's worship, and a time when people can come closer to God. There is a strong focus on Jesus: when we asked some of the new Christians in the church about Jesus, they told us how he had transformed their lives. It is worth repeating the words of the man who told us that when he took communion it was like "wires coming from upstairs [i.e. heaven or God] straight down to all different people all over the world and everybody's got their own wire connected to Jesus and especially so on Sundays". He felt that if he couldn't be at church on Sunday for some reason, it hurt: "It's not as in somebody's hit you or something like that but you've got a horrible feeling in your stomach that something's missing, somebody's taken something away."

Church C doesn't have its own building and meets in the Methodist church. This is a good example of Whitworth's communal mission, where he encourages churches to follow Jesus' example of forming new communities (Whitworth, 2008: 125). This church meets outside of the traditional Sunday morning, and it is principally made up of people who are or have been homeless. The church started off as a drop-in on Saturday morning with help from people from other churches, where they offer food parcels, coffee and cake, and opportunities for prayer. Originally, people who came to the drop-in were encouraged to go to attend churches in the town, but this didn't work. Although the churches wanted to welcome the homeless people, they struggled to support these people and to cope with the substance abuse and chaotic lives that often accompany homelessness. The homeless community needed a church community of their own, where it was understood that some people might turn up late, drunk or high.

Of course, these stories above also give examples of Whitworth's category of relational mission, as churches meet people's needs for "stable, meaningful, close relationships" (Whitworth, 2008: 127). One further example is research location E. This town had grown rapidly in the 1850s with the iron and steel industry. There had originally been some bigger houses for the factory managers, but these had been cleared in the 1960s and 1970s, along with lots of the poorer housing stock. The town is now home to a large population of asylum seekers: as the housing stock is so cheap in this town and so many properties are vacant, the Home Office's contractors place lots of asylum seekers here. The town's Anglican church, like those mentioned above, is incarnational, contextual and communal. In the summer of 2018, the church hosted a *Great Get Together* in memory of the murdered MP Jo Cox, and 400 people came along. The local butcher had given them a good rate on meat, and the vicar barbecued. People from the town's Hindu temple danced and brought Indian food, and people from different countries brought foods from their countries of origin. The church also hosts a foodbank, sessions with a family worker, cookery courses and more.

So perhaps we can claim, then, *It's the end of the world as we know it (and I feel fine)*. Christendom has come or is coming to an end, but if we are faithful to the full "Paschal Mystery" of the birth, life, death, resurrection and ascension of the Christ there is nothing to fear and we can be full of hope. The churches we visited in the North, where we had been told "something is happening", were engaged in Brueggemann's "intense practice of hope" (Brueggemann, 1997: 106), and experiencing some of that resurrection life which is available to us. In the next two chapters, we'll attempt to "thicken up" our understanding of what might be happening in these churches beyond Whitworth's categories, and what new life and growth looks like in the context of a post-Christendom North.

Questions for reflection

1. Does the Church today feel alien, and its story not understood by wider society? If so, how does this make you feel?
2. Where is your community in relation to the setting sun of Christendom? How light or dark is it and what is the evidence for your answer?
3. Can you think of ways that being on the margin might be exciting for the Church?
4. What might Brueggemann's "intense practice of hope" look like in your church?

CHAPTER 4

Research findings: Fragility and freedom in the fuzzy Church

We have been preparing the ground so far in this book for a presentation of our research findings in relation to what gospel is found in "flourishing" northern churches. In the Introduction we presented some of the data from both the survey and seven "field visits". We have then described why it is important to take a theological approach to regions such as the North, begun to think about the meaning of the North beyond its actual geography and shared with the reader the current "brutal reality" of the state of the English Church in the early twenty-first century. We shared some initial engagement with the responses our research churches have been making to that reality.

In this chapter, we will develop our research findings alongside what we now know about theology, the North and the dying of Christendom. This will enable us to make some positive, if tentative, assertions about what the gospel looks like at this point in history in this particular region of England. In the next chapter, we are going to "thicken up" these findings by combining our research observations into an imaginative journey around northern churches where "something is happening".

What we didn't find!

[failure] All research (whether in a laboratory or in a local church) proceeds by testing hypotheses, setting out with some hunches as to what might be happening and, by trying those hunches out, confirming, modifying or disconfirming their truth. We have therefore to be very ready to fail in

order to learn in research. Noting where we went wrong and what we didn't find is therefore a good place to start in presenting our research findings.

We made the point in the Introduction, but it is worth repeating here, that it was hard to describe any of the churches we researched as "flourishing", taken as meaning rapid and almost spontaneous development, such as happens to plant life in springtime. Even the larger ones, in terms of numbers, were working incredibly hard to keep those they had and grow relationally with the community around them. This is not to say that aspects of flourishing were not visible in the churches and in individual new Christians within them. It is also worth noting here that it is hard to avoid the organic or ecological metaphor for growth when discussing the life of local churches—a theme we will return to.

The idea of flourishing has a long theological pedigree going right back to the "abundant life" Jesus offers in John 10:10. My colleague from South Africa, Nelus Niemandt, describes how "flourishing life" has increasingly become a goal (or *telos*) of mission and evangelism across a broad ecumenical spectrum in recent decades (Niemandt, 2020). I suppose what we saw in our research churches were the first beginnings of growth rather than the later stage which might be described as flourishing. I'm a passionate gardener, and I know the most dangerous phase for plants is when they first emerge from the ground—and the slugs move in! One of the few other books written about mission in the North, from the particular perspective of Port Clarence on Teesside, is *Mission from Below: Growing a Kingdom Community* (Hodgson, 2018); its cover picture is of someone cupping a fragile plant in their hands before, presumably, planting it out (the book, by the way, affirms many of our findings in this research). When growth begins to happen, the soil begins to shift, and the good gardener knows something is happening and not to interfere just yet.[8]

---

[8] We plan another book on our research which will look in further critical depth at the research project and its outcomes. Part of this work will be to map the initial growth we have been discovering onto a set of "stages of growth" outlined in an important book on the subject by Stephen Spencer (2019: 93). Interestingly the title of Spencer's book also includes flourishing and an organic metaphor.

We have also alluded to the bigger "epic fail" in our research already—
the essentialist nature of our starting research question. We set out
thinking there might be some identifiable (even direct) correlation
between northern culture and the gospel which could be revealed in our
subject churches if we looked hard enough. We took the position that the
gospel (as we discussed in Chapter 1) isn't a fixed "thing" to be inserted
into the culture and the context (Bevans' translation model), but rather
it finds its place and life in "prophetic dialogue" with that culture, to use
the title of Bevans and Schroeder's later book (2011).

gospel

It is worth pointing out here as a slight digression, that while there
was evidence of the translation model being operative in some of our
research churches, especially amongst the leadership and in the preaching
and teaching we observed (this was particularly the case in the more
evangelical and charismatic churches, which is to be expected), there was
very little evidence of any "propositional" theology being repeated back to
us, by the new Christians in their focus groups. We'll detail more of what
was said below, but what was largely absent were creedal repetitions or
cognitive assertions about, for instance, how Jesus has "paid the penalty
for our sins". We intuitively, mostly (not in every case), kept the leadership
out of these focus groups and the data reveals the wisdom of that, for
it might have been a different matter if the new converts had felt they
needed to give the "right" answer.

nb

Yet we were overly confident about what Northernness arising from
context and as culture might be. We discovered it is much more complex
than we had thought, and we needed to explore it (as we did in Chapter
2) much more deeply and broadly to discover its ever-changing nature
and meaning at this particular time. In that exploration, we noted that
"affirmation and resistance" through authenticity, community and
humour are deeply embedded in an approach to Northernness which is
life-giving and therefore, we claim, gospel and kingdom-oriented, since
the North experiences coloniality as a region in England as a whole. The
relationship between faith and culture in northern churches is therefore
much more subtle, nuanced and complex than we had ever imagined. On
the far side of the research, however, it is difficult not to be embarrassed
by our initial stance—what else did we expect, but subtlety and nuance?
We believe then it is time to move on from what we didn't learn to what

we did and name the accented northern gospel which is evident in the research data.

The gospel in a northern dialect

In examining the data as we did, the first thing we noticed was that we could describe both the leaders and the new Christians in our research churches as down-to-earth, honest, real, inclusive and vulnerable. This chimes very much with two of the *Gehalt* themes in Northernness of authenticity and community.

Before moving on, and now we have had the importance of humour pointed out as the third of those themes, we can record that there are seventy-three occasions where the transcription of the focus groups notes *[laughter]* that there was laughter and six occasions where laughing is referred to by a speaker. We know that there are many different types of laughter, including the nervous, anxious sort which might be expected in an interview. Without doing a further detailed study of how each occasion of laughter sounded we can still suggest that this number of occasions is remarkable evidence for the importance of humour where something is happening related to the gospel and the kingdom. Our respondents, it seems, were having fun (perhaps even experiencing joy) participating in the life of God flowing amongst them.

Returning to authenticity, here is a new Christian from church A describing how they came to faith and what they would say about it to a stranger with deep honesty and, therefore, not a little vulnerability:

> I went through a really bad period in my life. I lost my grandfather who was a central figure in raising me, because my mum was poorly an awful lot of the time when I was a child, and my best friend committed suicide, and my wife died of cancer. And I drifted for quite a while, no real purpose, nothing to get up for, and when I became a Christian, I was able to put that down, and let Jesus have it, because some of it was really bad you know. You never want to look at the face of a man who's hung himself. And now, I live a life of purpose here on earth, and when I'm done,

I'll get called to my proper home, and there'll be a room for me. So that's what I would tell people about, how life has transformed and turned to face the sunlight.

We have already quoted the leader from church G in Chapter 2, but it is worth repeating here to emphasize the down-to-earth nature of ministry in the North:

But it's grounded-ness, isn't it? I don't know whether we're lucky because grounded-ness is easier in the North. Because obviously, I've lived in the South as well and . . . one of the huge differences about prayer in the prison is just that it is incredibly grounded and it's incredibly real.

In a set of northern rural churches (F) a leader made a direct connection between openness as a northern cultural trait and the task of mission (and this is possibly the only direct connection we came across in the data):

I think there's probably a distinctiveness about northern in that, it's like the sort of analogy of the northerner on the tube smiling and talking to people. I think that's what, if you're going to use that analogy, that's what, what we've, what I feel we're here to do. To open conversation with people, to introduce, just all of that.

In church B, when we asked the new Christians what they would say to someone they met about being a Christian, they were not being reticent or holding back. These were some of the responses (and note the reference to the strength of community as well):

Resp 1: Oh, I'd say imagine pleasure and times it by a thousand, thousand. [Laughs]

Resp 5: That's amazing. Can I steal that? I'll use that.

Resp 2: My life is as hard as yours but at least I'm not on my own.

Resp 3: I would say something along those lines, fear not, fear not.

A leader at church G spoke specifically about honesty in relation to the North and noticed its affirmation by someone who is "posh":

> I think there is, that's a northern thing, about people are much more open. I'm probably . . . probably a tad too open for them . . . well, I just can't help it, it's out and I think, "Well, no, it's about being honest." I've got a very, very dear friend who is very frightfully posh, [name], and she loves my family, she loves to come here because . . . she can be herself, she doesn't have to pretend.

Back with the leaders in church B we were discussing what they had said about themselves when the survey was filled in—which it turned out had been done solely by the vicar (we had suggested leadership teams might do it together). The leader had described them as a "real, honest, broad and welcoming Christian community". In repeating that back to the group, I asked whether they agreed with that statement, and this was the ensuing conversation:

> **Resp 4:** That sounds good to me.
> **Resp 1 (vicar):** Must have been a good day when I filled that in.
> **All:** [Laughs]
> **Resp 4:** I think he's right.
> **Resp 2:** I think he's right.
> **Interviewer:** What do you mean by honest?
> **Resp 4:** We're willing to say it's like it is.
> **Resp 1:** From the front, we're real and we're not . . .
> **Interviewer:** Give me an example of that.
> **Resp 1:** Well, I will, no, we will share our struggles as preachers, as hosts, as leaders. We will be real people, not that I've got it all sorted.
> **Resp 2:** As I say, absolutely what [vicar] said really, and it is the leadership of [vicar]. [vicar] is a vulnerable leader. He shares his vulnerabilities which encourages everybody else to share their vulnerabilities and that's life. That's what I mean by honest. It's that,

you know what, you see what you're getting, and people are open to
that.

Resp 3: Another example would be . . . when you get testimonies from
the front, it can also be at the end of the story and everything is
now wonderful, but we had a girl come up last week, who said, you
know, I'm on a journey out of addiction. I slipped recently but I'm
just telling you I'm back. And it wasn't like this is the end of the
story, but I'm here, I'm just being honest, and she felt secure enough
to say that in front of everybody else. That's amazing.

Once again, we can note in this conversation the connection between
being open, real and honest alongside including people who might
otherwise be outcasts of society since the "containment" the church and
its leadership provides is good enough for that honest sharing.

At church D a new Christian gave testimony to the sense of community
formed by the congregation:

When I came to [estate], about three years ago and being here has
changed me a lot of ways. Meeting a lot of lovely people, being a
part of the [church], being part of the choir and just really having
a church family and you know, when you feel low you can go to
people and someone's always there by your side. There's always
somebody you can turn to, or to be honest, sometimes you don't
even have to say anything they know, and they come to you and
to me that's amazing and I've tried to tell my family as well you
know.

Church F offered a fascinating discussion about the activity of God, fuzzy
boundaries and the formation of community. The conversation began
when the interviewer asked about what it was that was enabling people
to come to faith:

Resp 2: God.
Resp 1: It's probably true.
Resp 2: [laughter] Just hold onto us. It has to be God.

Resp 3: I think there's a bit of fluffy edges though that when I say people are coming to faith, it's quite hard to know when that is because there is no point at which they sign on the dotted line. But, but what we can see is people who didn't come to church, were not bothered about God, who now are and who will have conversations. So, I guess that's perhaps what we're talking about when we say coming to faith. There are not, not necessarily those overt signs but I, I, I think again it's a fuzzy edge about a few things, that it's about community and feeling part of something and belonging. And that's, it's a little bit to do with the village community but it's probably more to do with the church community.

The example of the recovering addict offering testimony leads us to a further key finding about the nature of faith and culture in our churches that emerged for us from the whole research project—that of "fragility and freedom". We have already noted in this chapter how flourishing was considered not to be the correct adjective to apply to these churches because of the fragile nature of what is growing in them. In church C, the designated overall leader described how the emerging congregation was able to hold people in the fragility of their lives while being free to welcome them "in and out", even while the worship liturgy was happening:

I think it's changed me to realize that everyone's accepted and significant and secure in God, and everyone's welcome. Yeah, and it is very different to other churches where, like you mentioned about people going out for a cigarette. Our guys sometimes they need to go out for a cigarette because they need a break, but they always come back, and they're welcomed back in. Yeah, it's very different. I think it's very important that they can feel welcomed in here if they go out, they can come back in and you know if they, they are under the influence of drugs they're still welcome, and God loves them as they are and gets them where they're at.

In church D, set in a very fragile, "deprived" in economic terms, estate community, where people were rejected even in the wider locality, the stance of the church at the Eucharist dealt with this fragility by offering what might be described as an "open-open table". No belief whatsoever is required for the reception of the consecrated elements (so it is not just baptism that is not required as in the "open table" stance)—in fact when I observed the worship, it seemed there was an innate expectation that everyone, no matter who they were, would participate. In both focus groups, this stance was affirmed first by someone who spoke about their experience of communion: "It's the closest you get to him [Jesus] because it's [the bread and wine] a part of him [silence]." Then the leadership confirmed this profound experience (which engendered silence) arising from the open table policy and said the diocesan bishops have visited and "they've been fine with it". As researchers, here we noticed the coming together of fragility and freedom at the very point liturgically and theologically when they might be best connected—at the Eucharist.

Eucharist

It is worth expanding a little further on the theme of freedom. Two of our seven churches had labelled themselves or a key community project with the word freedom. Two others either spoke eloquently about it or demonstrated it by placing a banner in their worship space proclaiming it. While the others may not have mentioned freedom *per se* it is clear the new Christians were finding freedom in their faith.

Church A made a direct link between a literal "free" event they were putting on, the kingdom and the community project named "Freedom" that arose from that first engagement:

> The very first thing that happened before it was Freedom, before it was a ministry; we had a week, and we had a marquee on a local community area, and the idea behind that was that the concept was, that people always expected the church to be asking for money, asking for things. And we wanted this week to be where the church gave. So, everything, for the whole week, it was morning, afternoon and evening, was free. So that's your "Free". And the fact at that time was that it was a church activity, so we were open that that would be a steppingstone into the king*dom*. So, it's "Free*dom*". Ok? [Laughter]

The other aspect of the accented gospel it is worth noting is how several of the churches and their leadership intentionally engaged with class as a cultural signifier and barrier. The best example was at church C where the largely middle-class leaders were discussing how they had been changed by working with people coming to receive food parcels and then that turning into a worshipping community:

> **Resp 1:** I suppose that at the beginning there was quite an element of fear involved with when you see these people, if they're all tattooed up and whatever it would be quite intimidating. So just having erm, to know how you are empowered by the Holy Spirit and who you are in Jesus to know that they're not intimidating, they're humans, they're, I don't know.
>
> **Resp 2:** Significant, yeah.
>
> **Resp 1:** And they're coming at their most vulnerable point, so it would be wrong of me to start saying, getting kind of offended of how they look and being afraid by it but just kind of embracing for who they are.
>
> **Interviewer:** So, your fear of the other is taken away then by meeting them and . . .
>
> **Resp 1:** Yeah because it, like growing up, I grew up in an Anglican church and a very middle-class family and not exposed to anything.
>
> **Interviewer:** In [same town]?
>
> **Resp 1:** Yeah, yeah not exposed to anything like that at all, a very good upbringing. And then to be kind of thrown into this, bam, it was like wow! It was yeah really a massive learning curve.
>
> **Resp 3:** Even for actually all three of us because none of us really had exposure to anything like the stuff that we were exposed to here . . . God didn't call us here because of the qualifications, do you know what I mean? They didn't call because we're qualified. But yeah in that sense we'd got no idea, had we? I don't know that we're that much better now.

There is more we could say about the accented northern gospel particularly around how leadership seemed to work in relation to the North, but that is probably best saved for Chapter 6 since it relates to the capacity of these churches to engage with their cultural and contextual realities. What remains in this chapter is to outline in slightly broader terms what good news is at the heart of the churches we researched, in order to offer some kind of response to our initial research question. Perhaps this is where readers beyond the North might want to take particular notice, since we suspect these characteristics of churches where something is happening might be more universally applicable (while remaining related to what we have already been noticing, as we'll see).

The good news at the heart of "something's happening" churches

There are three key points that need to be made here and we'll deal with two of them now; we'll leave what we noticed about the activity of God the Holy Spirit amongst the churches to our final chapter as we want to deal with that in more detail there. So here we'll look at how, in our churches, "everyone's welcome", and this leads to the church being changed by those joining it. Second, we'll think about who Jesus was for the people coming to faith in the churches, given our hunch that Jesus and the gospel are very closely connected theologically.

We have already noted how at church C the leadership had to cross a class boundary to meet and share worship with those who looked very different to themselves. They also recognized they were still on that journey.

Here is another reflection from church G, where the boundary being crossed is ethnicity:

> **Resp 1:** I remember the first week that there was quite a lot of Iranians here. I went . . . they were just all sat in the pews, and I just went up to them and said, "Hello, welcome", and they were so . . . . "Why are you so happy to see us?" Actually, was the question, "Why are *you* so happy to see us?" And I said, "Well, I think it's marvellous that they've come to this church to meet us." In fact, I was thanking them for coming and they were absolutely amazed that we were embracing them and saying.
>
> **Resp 2:** And I think that is something that has changed because when we first came here it was a really white . . .

Resp 1: Oh, it was.

Resp 2: Kind of population. And to be honest, when we first had people who were a little different to the established congregation, some people weren't so happy, and we had to . . .

Resp 1: True.

Resp 2: But I think what we found over recent years and stuff is . . . I know you've said this quite a lot, [name], that we've really received from and been blessed by the new people who have come in.

Resp 1: They have actually changed us, changed our . . .

Resp 3: Attitude.

Resp 2: Changed that British . . . don't come too close, kind of thing. They . . . just throw their trust at us and I kept thinking, "My God, what some of them have been through and they can accept that I'm going to be their friend."

I don't know of any church in England that does not espouse a theology of welcome—most church noticeboards proclaim this loudly and clearly. And yet from my work with the Church Mission Society on helping churches to change their culture I also know that it is quite difficult to join a church *if you don't look like the majority of the existing congregation in age, class, ethnicity or other identity markers.* What tends to happen (and I have research data which backs this up) is that God is always sending new people to churches, and they are welcomed with open arms—for a week or two. But if they don't "fit" they drift away, frozen out by the existing members who don't do this deliberately, yet unconsciously they offer all sorts of "you're not welcome" signals. What is different about the majority of our research churches is that there is solid evidence that they offer a more *radical welcome.* Thus, beyond the usual rhetoric of welcome they are genuinely open and receptive to the "other" and therefore to being changed by their presence among them.

There are several ways to understand the importance of this phenomenon, and we'll mention a few here. But first some more examples from our research data.

Continuing at church C where the respondent became noticeably emotional about the church's stance of radical welcome:

That's what drew me to this place, just no-one is kept out, nobody is kept away. Everybody is invited and welcomed into this. That's really what got through to me and everybody is welcome in this place. It doesn't matter who they are, what they're doing, where they're at, there [are] just open arms here. That's really what drew me into this place.

Church D's strapline includes the fact that "everyone's welcome", *and* they embody this vision in action:

We, we make a point of everybody knowing that everybody is welcome. Erm, we had a lady, we won't name names, but we had a lady who has got some real battles with demons and mental health going on, and she used to come to our Bible study here on a Thursday. Erm, and some of the stuff that she would come out with is crazy stuff, but actually it's okay to have that opinion. It's alright to feel that way if that's the way you feel. We're not going to say that that's wrong . . .

At church E the leaders were discussing how people came to faith and stayed:

Resp 1: I think it's just the welcome of everybody here makes someone to feel . . . well, allows them to feel they can come back and know more. Then I think when you started doing Pilgrim courses to help them explore more about what and who God is all about.

Resp 2: Yes. I think fundamentally, it has not been anything particularly complicated, it has been the welcome. And it's more than welcome, it's about authentic Christian community that what they say and how they act are of a piece. It's not perfect but there is an integrity about that.

Finally, at church G a respondent recognizes that a culture of inclusive welcome comes from the stance and holding capacity of the leadership:

But it's that welcome isn't it, and that fellowship that people can feel like they are in a safe space, that they can come and be themselves and people will accept them for who they are. I don't think that's a given in any place, I think that is because of our congregations and the way that they are. And I think it comes from the leadership as well that we are welcoming and inclusive.

A much more thorough-going and theological study of the phenomenon we are describing here is Al Barrett and Ruth Harley's 2020 book *Being Interrupted* (which in turn is a practical outworking of Barrett's doctoral thesis published as *Interrupting the Church's Flow* (2020)) based on the work of the church in Hodge Hill, Birmingham. There is much more depth and breadth in that book about the basic movement we are describing here. The key idea in Barrett and Harley's work is that the church is renewed not by "flowing" outwards into its community (in order to "get people back into church"), but by being "interrupted" with a flow in the opposite direction. We suggest this is also what we have noticed in our research churches: they embrace the interruption that their newcomers bring.

Connected to this are the concepts of *adaptive* leadership and change attributable to Ron Heifetz (2009) and adopted in my own work in congregational culture change. Heifetz describes the difference between technical and adaptive problems. A technical problem, like the church boiler breaking, has a technical fix which can be applied to it. But nothing in the church needs to change for that to happen. A bunch of Iranian asylum seekers turning up in church or homeless people asking for prayer and worship and finding healing are *adaptive* challenges which, if they are responded to faithfully, will change those dealing with them, as we have seen. If churches want to change, they need to seek out, or to put it more theologically, discern adaptive challenges which God is sending them from their community (their interruptions) and address them in vulnerability and not knowing (or *conscious incompetence* as we like to call it).

Therefore, it really helps if churches understand themselves as human organizations which are open systems. There is a whole set of theories associated with open systems which I have written about elsewhere

(Rooms 2019; Rooms & Keifert 2019), and I'll simply summarize briefly here. All living organisms that are alive have semi-permeable boundaries across which *inputs* and *outputs* can pass. The inputs are transformed into outputs within the system and then go on to create *outcomes* in the context of the system outside it, which can then turn into new inputs. This cycle can become virtuous which is when the organism grows. If the boundary to the outside becomes too thick or impervious, the organism will die. Churches are much the same: the resources for their future are found outside of them in their context (yet another reason for taking context seriously theologically!) not within themselves. Again, our data has shown the "fuzzy" boundaries of many of the churches we studied. One of them (F) used that very word for what they had created, as we noted above and have now fully owned in the title of the book. Earlier in this chapter we mentioned the use of organic metaphors for how churches behave and here we can see how that growth begins to happen—a leader in the Fresh Expressions movement, Graham Cray, coined the phrase "walls down, roots down" for this very movement. Further research by the Theos Think Tank and the Church Urban Fund (Rich, 2020) in more than sixty parishes and 350 interviews over three years (a much bigger project than ours) also confirms the relationship between what they call "social action" (and what we would call creating fuzzy boundaries, open systems), discipleship and church growth. The executive summary of the research report states that:

> Social action can be a route to church growth in both numerical and spiritual terms. Further, social action is one of the key ways in which congregations can build wider networks of relationships resulting in people initiating a faith journey and joining the church. Crucially, social action leads to church growth when it enables congregations to develop meaningful relationships with those they would not otherwise have done, or who might not otherwise have come into sustained contact with the church.

Finally, we'll look at who Jesus is in our research churches on the basis that Christianity is a faith based on the incarnation. It is therefore rooted, first of all, in a person, not a set of ideas from a book (as we noted in the Introduction, we were encouraged in this line of inquiry in our conversation with the missiologist, Steve Bevans).

Let's start with the survey data across eighteen churches (not all answered the question fully) who we asked to describe Jesus in five words. Out of the eighty-four responses the most frequent was friend (10) followed by variations on love (7) and saviour (7). There were five mentions of Jesus as Lord and interestingly, given the discussion above, five who named Jesus as "accepting" of everyone and non-judgmental. Next were teacher (4), healer (3), kind (2), King (2), alive (2), challenging (2) and forgiving (2). Of the thirty-three single occurrences we think some of the ones of note for our research are liberator, restorer, real, down-to-earth and joy-giving.

We also analysed, with a particular methodology, the 278 places that Jesus was mentioned in the focus groups with the new Christians. Without going into too much detail here, we found four themes arising from this analysis, with the most frequently occurring theme at the top (much of which reinforces the survey data):

Jesus is someone we can have a personal relationship with.
Jesus is a friend; someone we can feel at home/be at one with; someone you can talk to personally; even like a spouse and someone you could cuddle. Jesus is reliable, protective and trustworthy; knowing Jesus made our participants happy; they felt peace, contentment, joy, excited and euphoric in their relationships with Jesus; there was a strong sense that Jesus accepted them as they were.

Jesus is someone who changes us.
Participants felt that Jesus had changed them, for example: to grow into a better person; to love and help others; to be free from addiction; to have a sense of purpose; to love and be happy; to help them by pulling them back when they were going to do something wrong. Overall, we sensed that they thought Jesus was changing them to make them more like Jesus.

Jesus is God.
Less frequently occurring was the sense of Jesus as God, as divine, or as supernatural.

When Jesus was talked about in this way, our participants talked about Jesus as: a saviour; a higher being; the hope on earth; someone who heals, miraculously; someone you can pray to, and who answers prayer.

Jesus is someone known in community.

Jesus was known also as someone in community with others; someone who chooses to be with people; someone who would have people all around him; the centre of it all; part of the action; someone who might listen to others, taking it all in and enjoying it.

The main point that arises for us from this extensive data is that Jesus emerges as *both* a personal, private Jesus (friend, protector, lover) *and* a public Christ (saviour, Lord, God). In fact, we can note the progression from the private to the public Jesus Christ in the descriptions of Jesus derived from the focus group conversations. It is worth sharing some particular examples of this interplay of the personal and public Christ.

At church A here is a respondent extending the personal, caring Jesus to be something worth sharing more widely:

> Jesus cares for you, and He's influenced the people in the church to pass that on. That there's always somebody there, you can pray to Jesus, but He's always encouraged people in the church to do what He was doing, and to carry on that Word.

A respondent at church B had returned to faith after falling out with the church in the past. The vicar had offered some counselling support which was taken up and then:

> So, yeah, I had a few sessions with this lass, and one day I was out with my car, and I just felt this overwhelming love that I was loved, and not only was Jesus bothered about whether I was Christian, he was worried about my little individual struggles like living in the house with no Christians. Basically, what I'm trying to say is they [the church] cared enough about me, to put me back on the straight path . . .

Thus, the personal experience of God is understood within the actions of the whole people of God in community. In church G, a respondent had picked a picture of a football crowd scene:

> At the . . . crowd there is this guy holding up a thing that says, "Brendan, I've got your back," and I like that because I think Jesus has got our back, and I think he's got our back in a way that people who love us always have. Because even though there was no . . . that we make mistakes, we've got lots of faults, we get it wrong, we can be selfish. But they can see something in us that makes them still love us and it's very comforting to know that, it's very interesting. And also, he's in the middle of a crowd and Jesus always seemed to be in the middle of a crowd, didn't he? And he is with lots of ordinary people, and he's quite happy, that's his place, he's chosen to be there. So, I quite like that.

Once again, the personal, private sense of Jesus having our back is mixed with the public nature of that stance within a crowd. A final quote sums this attitude to Jesus up the best and came from a later section, when we asked people in church G to describe what Jesus would look like if he appeared "round here" today:

> Somebody that you feel, you know, is just part of this community that you can just relate to. You would feel comfortable sitting next to him on a bus, just to chat, and I think somebody, who is probably quite . . . they don't offer lots of words, but you can tell they're interested in you and maybe over listening conversations that imagine if you were sitting in church, just taking it all in and enjoying it.

The period of what is known as modernity or the Enlightenment (around 1650–1950), which is now coming to an end (along with Christendom; the two are connected), split up the private and public realms in our lives as Western people. Religion was relegated (as a value-laden activity) to the private sphere, while the "factual" nature of science and technology reigned in public. The Church both institutionally and locally rather gave in to this state of affairs, such that again I have research evidence which shows that churches now rarely take public action in the name of the church—they rely on private individuals being involved in their communities. However, we have seen in this research and elsewhere that when the Church as a whole body begins to act in public across its boundary, it comes alive. Our data about the personal/private and public Christ available in northern churches where something is happening confirms this reality.

We would expect what is known elsewhere after the work of Parker Palmer (1981) as the "ideology of intimacy" to be present in these churches, and indeed it is. The importance of Jesus as friend and the church as family is noticeable throughout our data. Pat Keifert addresses this phenomenon head-on in his important work *Welcoming the Stranger* (1992), and it is clear that our churches have learnt how to break some of that ideology down by worshipping and following a public Christ into the world (and on the bus), which enables them to welcome the stranger in their midst.

In conclusion then, we can describe our research churches as "Fuzzy Church"—they have learnt how to create a fuzzy boundary at their edge, to be changed by those who are joining them and to witness to a public, transformational Christ within the world around them. This is good news, gospel arising authentically from who they are and who they are becoming.

Questions for reflection

1. What stands out most to you from our research findings in this chapter? Why do you think this factor has caught your attention so strongly?
2. If you could change one thing about your own church as a result of reading this chapter what might it be?
3. Where, if at all, are the interruptions coming from which might be of God in your context?
4. How does the local church stand up and take its place as a corporate entity in public in the community it finds itself in?

CHAPTER 5

"Let me take you by the hand . . . "

This chapter is a bit different to all the others in this book. The title of the chapter references a popular and much-covered folk song from the 1970s originally penned by Ralph McTell called "Streets of London", which we transpose to the North. Its original purpose was to make "the unknown known" (see Chapters 2 and 6) regarding the state of the street homeless. We'd like to take you, the reader, by the hand to have a look around the churches we researched—to paint an imaginative picture of them which we hope will "thicken" the research we are presenting and enable you to "stand in the shoes" a bit more of those who worship in them. These imaginative sketches are conglomerated from the notes we took on the field research trips. We've done our absolute best to mix them up so that none of them can be identified as we promised anonymity to all our respondents (and all the names have been changed). The point is not to try and identify any of the churches (even if you, the reader, were a member of any of them!), rather their contexts, behaviours and stories are presented here in this way so that you can compare and contrast them with your own situation and learn from them. Imagine we are "taking you by the hand" and leading you imaginatively around some northern churches that we know on a single day.

It's a cold, clear Sunday morning, just at the end of winter. You're going to church, the 10.30 communion service at an Anglican church. The church is an old Victorian building, darkened with soot and pollution from a previous era, and buddleias are in abundance in the gutters, blackened too from the rigours of winter. The PCC have considered closing the church several times over the last few decades: the building costs more money to maintain than they can afford. The archdeacon often asks the vicar why they aren't giving more money to the diocese, given that people are coming to faith through the church, but although these new people often volunteer their time for the church, they simply don't have much money to give.

The church is in a town in the North of England: not in the centre of the town, but on an outer estate. The town received some regeneration funding and government investment in the 1990s and early 2000s, but none of that money reached this estate. There used to be a factory at the end of the road the church is on, but that closed thirty-five years ago. The terraced houses on the estate are now in bad repair. Most of them are houses of multiple occupancy owned by landlords who live hundreds of miles away.

Inside the church, there's the remnants of breakfast being cleared away. One of the churchwardens brings flasks of tea and coffee and makes up hot bacon butties for the breakfast club that happens before the service. Another churchwarden hands you the order of service and pew sheet: on the front there's a list of all the activities the church holds throughout the week. There's a lot going on! You're surprised that there's a young people's Bible study group one evening. Then there's the foodbank, the "mums and tots" group, a cycling club out on a trip next Saturday, a community choir and a lunch club with communion for older men. The last of these began as a lunch club for lonely older men in the community, but after they'd been meeting for a few months, the men asked if they could have communion as well. They felt that the lunch club had become their church. You notice what a powerful sign this must be to the church of people making their voice heard about what they want and permission being given for that to go ahead. You wonder how frequent an experience like that is, for people around here.

At the front of the church, there's a "light a candle" sign and tea lights on a stand. A few candles are already alight, and a woman behind you goes up, telling her neighbour, "I'm going to light one for my mother." There's a children's area beneath the pulpit on the floor with a mat, toys, and balls that are already being thrown around by the gathering children. It's clearly a well-used space. There's a PowerPoint presentation on a screen, with welcome notices in English, Arabic, French and Yoruba.

This makes you curious about the congregation that gathers here and how these different people and languages meet and interact.

The people in the church are pretty mixed: there are some older, local people, some young families, and a fair few asylum seekers from Syria and different parts of Africa, which makes sense given the notices. There's a couple, Mohammed and Amira, who come with their two young daughters. Amira first had contact with the church when a friend told her they had free clothes and toys for children. She couldn't believe they were giving things away for free. She and Mohammed wanted to find out more about why the Christians would do this, and they converted five months ago. As the father of daughters, Mohammed loves that women and men are more equal in Christianity than they are in Islam.

Sylvia, one of the churchwardens, feels really honoured that Mohammed, Amira and their fellow asylum seekers come to their church. She remembers the first time she met Mohammed and Amira: she'd gone to say hello and welcome them, and they had seemed so confused and amazed that Sylvia was happy to see them there. There had been a few older church members who weren't sure at first, but now the Syrians and Africans are part of the church. Sylvia's only regret is that so many of them have to move on when they're granted asylum.

The service starts with a small procession of the cross, two servers with candles, and the priest, Barbara. Barbara grew up in the town. She moved away to a neighbouring city in her twenties, and did her ordination training down south, in her forties. She's married to Mick, who's a police officer, and he's training to be a Reader. She loves being a vicar in her hometown: she feels she really understands the people she's serving. Kathy is one of the servers holding a candle and wearing a robe. It's been hard for her to get to church this morning, as her depression is really bad at the moment. She met Barbara when her son died, and Barbara took the funeral. She likes having a job to do at church; it helps her feel needed. She and Barbara text each other every day.

The communion service is pretty traditional, following Anglican *Common Worship*. Barbara gives a brief explanation of what every part of the service is, using language everyone can understand. She doesn't use the word "collect", but instead introduces the "special prayer for today". Some of the songs in the service are more traditional hymns, like "Be thou my vision", and there are a couple of more modern songs, like "Who you say I am" from Hillsong music. The New Testament reading is read by one of the children, Chloe. Chloe does a good job—there's a few long words in the reading—and the congregation give her a small round of applause at the end.

Barbara's sermon is all about freedom, and the freedom that we have in Christ. She preaches for ten minutes, only occasionally looking down at her notes. She often asks the congregation questions: what does freedom mean to them, what freedom has Jesus brought them? Freedom is an important theme for the whole church: Barbara often talks about it, and it's a familiar idea to the congregation. It feels to you like this notion of freedom stands over against some negative forces in this place and community, forces that shut people down and count them out.

The intercessions are led by Ray, who was born and bred in the town. He leads prayers for the work of the church, victims of a recent earthquake in India, people caught up in wars around the world, and for people who are struggling in the local area. There's something quite beautiful in the preciseness of the prayers which seem grounded in the particularities of the local and at the same time raising the congregation's horizons to the global.

When you go up for communion, Simon is on your right at the altar. He started coming to the church a year ago with his wife and kids. He's had a pretty rough life: he joined the army at sixteen, took drugs, drank far too much. But now Sunday's his favourite time of the week: if he doesn't come to church, it gives him a horrible feeling in his stomach. He feels Jesus has helped him be a better person, a better father, a better husband. Jesus is the second most important person in his life, after his wife. He imagines his relationship with God as like a wire coming down from upstairs, straight down to all different people all over the world, and he feels his wire, his connection to Jesus most strongly when he's taking communion.

At the end of the service, Barbara introduces the notices. It's the turn of Chantelle, the other churchwarden, to come up and tell the congregation what's going on during the week. The gardening club has been moved from 10 a.m. on Tuesday to 11 a.m. (you're amazed as this happening didn't get a mention on the official printed notice sheet—another thing to add to the list). Chantelle is leading mums and tots this week, they'll be praying using a bubble tube. Mohammed is starting an Alpha course in Arabic for the Syrians. The notices aren't really just notices, you realize quickly; it's a time for the congregation to celebrate what they do, and share what's been going on. There is a pride and a "standing tall" in the notice-givers as they come forward. Chantelle lets the congregation know that one of their foodbank regulars asked for prayer for healing from addiction this week: the congregation are delighted.

And Chantelle has even more exciting news: Farid has been granted asylum. He and Mohammed come up to the front, where Farid thanks everyone in church for helping him, and Mohammed translates what he says from Arabic to English. Farid shares how God has helped him through the difficulties of the asylum process and asks people to pray for him. His accommodation in the town will now be taken back from him, and he's going to join a cousin on the other side of the country. Farid says he'll miss everyone at church. You intuit a sense of solidarity and relief arising across the pews as this news is shared; it seems people here know the government does not grant asylum easily, which adds to the sense that Farid has been "held" by his sisters and brothers in his long quest. You notice there have been two quite different "healings" going on.

The service ends with the cross, servers, and Barbara processing to the back of church, where she blesses the congregation, and reminds them to stay for tea and coffee in the hall. You join them all in the hall: the cakes are baked by members of the congregation, and are excellent, there's a buzz you notice and people talking across lots of traditional divides of class, gender and race which again surprises you. You wonder what this congregation might look like in five or ten years' time if it continues to grow in this slow and steady fashion.

———

In the afternoon there's a service with a very different vibe, but no less energy, in a "satellite village" just outside the town and definitely in the countryside. The service has a non-denominational feel since it's run by people from different churches who form the leadership team and are clearly influenced by the charismatic movement. The fact that it takes place in a local government community centre rather than a church building, and the timing, all add to the sense that something different is being attempted here away from "traditional" church. As you enter, the global hits the local on the screens at the front, as worship songs and then an American Christian stand-up comedian "entertain" the gathering throng while a small clock in the corner of the screen counts down the time to the start of the service—which begins exactly on time. During this time, you notice that the windows to the outside have been shaded and the lighting is subtle and focused on the leaders of worship. Various banners hang around the walls and one simply proclaims "Freedom". There's an area for the children at the back, and they seem able to play amongst themselves or participate in the worship as they prefer.

The leadership team is definitely "in charge", and there is a clear programme being worked: someone tells you that when they have communion, it happens first in the service, so that more time can be given to teaching, and they have also tried sharing it alongside the food that is always served after the service. There's just time to reflect on what a mixture of cultures, Christian traditions and influences there seems to be going on here all at the same time—and all this even before the worship has begun.

The leader begins the service with an "open mike" time and invites members to come up and share "what God has been up to" during the week. A mixture of people come up, but they are mainly the ones, you later find out, who are associated with some kind of leadership of the event. Nevertheless, several stories of conversion and healing draw you in by the way they are told to cries of "Amen!" You make a connection with what happened in the notices in the morning and realize that "public testimony" is a powerful element of the liturgy here. A string of contemporary worship songs led by a very professional band and "worship leader" follows. Later you meet this worship leader and realize they are given a status almost on a par with the lead minister. A programme of regular teaching through the sermon time is introduced. Today it is teaching about the kingdom of God and the preacher has clearly been working on the message for a lot of the week: the PowerPoint slides match up well, and it is recorded on video for those who weren't able to make it. What is interesting is that despite it being quite long, twenty minutes or so, and the way it includes a foray into the origins of "kingdom theology" in the Old Testament, the people mostly pay attention throughout. It makes you wonder if actually, because many are relatively new to faith, they are keen to learn and that's why they pay close attention to what is being taught. The formal prayers are a bit squeezed out since "there's not much time left now" and focus mainly on the life of this congregation and its community—however, there is an opportunity for the "ministry of prayer and healing" after the service for those who wish it.

Food is important in the life of this congregation—a simple, but hot meal is served after the service (there is a suitable hiatus between the two as people gather in a different space in the community centre for the meal) and the vast majority of people stay on afterwards. It is a major commitment from those cooking the food, but they seem up for serving in this way. Once again there's a buzz as people meet and catch up with each other.

—

In the evening, you go to a third church, a bit closer into the town centre, a Methodist church. The Methodist church has a long history in the town and the one you're visiting is a combination of two churches: some of the older members of the congregation still call it by its old name. It is located up a side street but remains quite visible.

You are welcomed into the church and step in from the cold evening. The space is rather dark, even a bit dingy, with wooden panelling, traditional pews and poor lighting. Plans have been made and money is being raised to reorder the interior later in the year. There is a recessed high table placed centrally as the focus with a cross on the table, all in the same wood. Two large chairs are placed either side of the table. There are professionally printed banners on the walls which brighten up the wood: one declares "Freely you have received . . . freely give". Like the Anglican church this morning and the banner at the afternoon worship, freedom is a big theme here.

To the left is a pulpit which isn't used in the service, and on the right is a raised stage with a microphone stand and small lectern, and it's from here that the service is led. To the right of that is the worship band, which consists of three men on guitar, drums and keyboard and two younger women singers. One of these singers is Fleur: she's back in the town at the moment, but will be going back to university down south again soon. She'd come to faith while doing her A levels; the congregation love to see her back and are glad that she's kept the connection with church despite going to uni. Fleur helps out with the Saturday food parcel drop-in when she's back at home. The band have been gently playing before the service, either practising or creating an atmosphere conducive to worship.

The service starts at 6.30 p.m., and there are about forty people now seated. Carol, the chief steward, opens the service. She's born and bred in the town and has lived there for seventy-five years. She also leads the Open the Book team who do assemblies at the local school, and the Messy Church that takes place on Tuesday after school. Carol tells the congregation a bit about the recent district synod, reminding people about the wider Methodist church family that this church is part of. She then hands over to Dan, the minister, to lead the worship.

Dan's originally from Scotland and has been part of this circuit for five years. Since he left Scotland fifteen years ago, he's always ministered in the North of England. He has helped the church think about what they can do to help people in their community who are homeless, and the church has started a Saturday drop-in in the church hall where homeless or vulnerably housed people can collect a food parcel for the week, as well as things like toothbrushes and toothpaste. There are tables where people can get a cup of tea and a fried breakfast, and a quiet room at the side where two church members pray for people, if they want prayer. There are also kids' activities in the church while their parents get a food parcel: Dan wanted the kids to think of the Saturday mornings as a time for fun. The children aren't aware that they're really there for their family to get some food for the week. The kids' activities are run by Lindsay: she's not a member of the church, in fact she says she is Pagan—and a white witch. But she wants to help the community and is happy to work with the church to do it. Carol and some of the other congregation members aren't happy with Lindsay's involvement, but Dan is keen to make sure anyone can join in to help the homeless and vulnerable families in the town. This is arresting for you—the boundaries of this church seem quite fluid then, and you wonder how Dan holds it all together.

Dan introduces two songs, and the congregational singing is loud and melodic. The church is part of a wider formal Ecumenical Partnership, and there's a standing joke in the Partnership that the Methodists are much better singers than the Anglicans. Dan then prays, and the church goes very quiet. He leads an extempore confession and absolution which leads into the Lord's Prayer. One of the kids in the congregation says a loud "Amen!" at the end, and Dan points her out as a great example. The collection is taken, and notices are given about the result of fundraising for flood relief in Africa, and an exciting donation from a Methodist fund towards the reordering of the building.

Then, there's time for testimonies. Tina takes the microphone and tells the congregation about how God is making connections in the town. She describes how she played the role of Santa's elf at an event over Christmas, where she made connections with the town's youth club. It seems that the club needs a new home, there's some funding available from the council, and there's a possibility that their church might be used as a base for the town's youth club. The congregation give some appreciative "oohs", and Tina tells them that "God connects things together". Dan affirms Tina's work, and tells the congregation that it is availability not ability that matters to God. That's three times you note in each of these churches that handing over the microphone at the front becomes such a powerful symbol for those being given permission to speak.

Dan introduces the Bible readings by saying that we are called to love our community, and we should look for unity and reconciliation, especially in the light of Brexit. We need to listen and learn to say sorry. He mentions this again in the prayers after the readings, as well as leading prayer for Israel, Palestine, Syria, Sierra Leone, Zimbabwe, and people in the town who are trapped by the effects of government policy, poverty and Universal Credit.

In his sermon, Dan shares the story of a woman he met in hospital who told him how a holding cross had helped her face her fears. He asks the congregation what the cross means to them and asks you to discuss this with your neighbour: you're sitting next to Andy. Andy initially came into contact with the church through their Saturday food parcel service, when he was homeless. Andy used to come for the food, a cup of tea and a dry place to chat to his friends, but one day he asked the prayer team to pray for him, and things just went from there. He's seen some amazing things happen with God. He's got a friend who's still using heroin and his needle marks on his arms had got infected: Dan prayed for his friend on the street, and the next day his friend's arms were healed. Andy now helps out at the Saturday drop-in, and the church are hoping that next year they can use their large basement as a night shelter in the winter. He tells you what the cross means to him: since finding out about Jesus, Andy feels his life has a purpose. When he's done here on earth, he'll get called to his proper home, and there'll be a room for him. It feels like his life's been turned around to face the sunlight.

In his sermon, one of the points Dan makes about the cross is how it helps us be reconciled. He brings in the story of David and Goliath. He describes how there were three ways of fighting at the time, with cavalry, sword or slingshot. Although David can't wear the sword-fighting armour as it doesn't fit, the slingshot was a still very serious weapon: Dan tells the congregation there was a Roman tool for removing the stones from the dead bodies of its victims. He turns around the story and describes how Goliath's bigness helped David: it's not that Goliath is so big David has no chance, Goliath is so big David can't miss! The congregation laugh at this, and Dan explains that it's the same with the cross. Although no-one gets it or sees the reality, God is reconciling on the cross.

There is a final prayer, and then the last hymn. There's a prayer team available for those who wish to be prayed for and coffee is served in the adjacent hall. You decline a cup after a long and fascinating day and walk out into the cold night, catching the first scent of spring growth in the air. So much to think about and reflect on now . . . so many common themes in these living churches string your experience of the day together—food, freedom, fluid boundaries, healing, testimony and the mixing up of many things into an amazing brew.

CHAPTER 6

Towards a northern contextual theology: The compost of the future Church

Our sense is that, as we move towards the end of the book, we can begin to present a vision of how things might be in churches that wish to flourish "after Christendom" in the light of our overall research. So, in this chapter, we'll take a step back from the detailed data that we have presented and share what we think are the implications of this study for a contemporary, even "post-colonial", contextual theology of the North of England and its churches. We'll then complete the book with a final theological chapter focusing on how we are making sense of the work of God, the Holy Spirit, in the places where something's happening.

Some years ago, and I forget where,[9] I came across a conversation that was aired when a religious order of nuns was facing the end of their life as a community, and they were thinking about how to end in the best way all they had been. When asked how the few nuns who were left thought of themselves and the resources they were left with, they said joyfully something like: "Oh, that's easy, we're the compost for whatever comes next." We have used ecological metaphors throughout this book for how Christian communities can be understood, and here is the same one popping up again in a different form. Inevitably we're not the only authors to do this—for example Al Barrett uses the compost analogy in a slightly different way in *Interrupting the Church's*

---

[9] Though it may have been with Dr Catherine Sexton, who was researching female religious orders for her doctorate which became *Theologies of ministry among older Roman Catholic sisters in the UK* (Cambridge: Anglia Ruskin University, 2018).

compost

Flow (2020: 207–12). Well-rotted compost or manure is the gold of the garden: without returning the goodness it contains, the soil becomes increasingly infertile. Even compost, however, needs careful stewarding to work at its best for the gardener. It helps if it is made up of different types of plant matter, which are collected together in one place and left for a suitable period for the microbes and worms to do their work, while being turned occasionally for aeration, before it is ready to restore its life-giving properties to the soil.

What we are going to suggest in this chapter is that there is a life-giving compost to be made from the post-modern, post-industrial, post-Christendom and post-colonial North. We have described that context from our perspective in Chapters 2 through 5. We've seen Christian faith become isolated at the top of a cultural "hill" as it finds itself as one option among many in a pluralist world, alongside the church coming out from behind its walls, becoming fuzzy at its boundary and therefore finding new life. We have visited post-industrial towns and cities where sometimes regeneration and repurposing has been possible, but more often than not the potential compost is just left rotting where it fell. There is more that could be said about that, and for an excellent survey of the signs of the times in England we would point the reader to the first chapters of *Being Interrupted* (2020), which delineate the societal issues we face post-Brexit, economically and in relation to race and the climate crisis. We have felt the othering of the North and the affirmation and resistance that is required to turn its inherited coloniality into the stuff of the kingdom of God. We'll need to be intentional and proactive, therefore, to make the best compost from the dying of many things which gave the Church a place in a world that has now passed. We claim that we have evidence from our research churches on how to go about this, since resurrection seems possible, however fragile it might be.

We'll have at least three main conversation partners in this chapter, all of whom we have already met briefly. Paul Bickley is a fellow researcher who authored one of the few other books about churches in a northern context in 2018, although it is more of a "research report". Al Barrett and Ruth Harley propose a method for creating life-giving compost while being faithful to the cross and resurrection in Chapters 15 and 16 of their book *Being Interrupted* (2020) with an extensive list of words beginning with r, and we will pick some of these up from time to time. Finally, we'll expand on Robert Heaney's (2019) proposals for a post-colonial theology beyond those we have already touched on in Chapter 2. In fact, let us begin with Heaney.

We have already mentioned two of Heaney's five characteristics of a post-colonial theology: coloniality and resistance. Coloniality, the reader may remember, is the ongoing suppression of people and their culture, which may not now be under full-blown colonialism, but nevertheless is still subjugated. In relation to our study we have noted how, to employ Heaney's definition (2019: 3), the South has historically assumed, and continues to assume "itself superior to already existing social, political, or cultural arrangements." We have also discovered how resistance to this state of affairs is an appropriate, even Christian response to othering beyond growing the hard, northern chip on the shoulder.

The other three characteristics are particularity, theological agency (and we might say simply agency *per se*) and hybridization. Particularity is about location and interestingly is the first of Barrett and Harley's moves too—they speak of relocation (2020: 174–5). We have emphasized the particularity of context throughout this book and located ourselves as researchers in relation to the North. However, there is more to be said and understood about the location of ourselves as authors, the leaders in our research churches and their physical, built environments. It is not surprising that very little has been written theologically about the North in England—this is Heaney's point regarding theological agency: the colonized disappear, are invisible in a world where theology is generated by the powerful. As we have pointed out before, the very existence of this research and the work we are presenting in this book goes some way to recovering the theological agency of the North. Hybridization, in Heaney's terms, is about how the culture, language, thought forms and behaviours of the colonized and the colonizers become mixed up—often in a deliberate attempt at subversion. We saw a version of this going on in Chapter 2 when discussing how northern comics can find a place amongst southern audiences. In relation to this study, hybridization, we think, gives us another angle to look at the "fuzzy" church we discovered in Chapter 4.

So, we will examine in detail, either again or for the first time, these five ways of approaching a nuanced post-colonial contextual theology from the North of England.

Particularity

Given that Christianity is a faith based on one particular person being born in a particular time and place it is not surprising that we have to take location utterly seriously. Yet the history of the Church in Christendom, as we have seen, has a much greater universalizing tendency than localizing one. Recovering location has to be part of the post-colonial project, according to Heaney, and we would wholeheartedly agree. When the church dies in a place, as we have noted it did in the location of church D, Christian presence is significantly reduced. While the local church cannot be reduced to the ordained trained professionals, the one thing that Anglican and Methodist churches have got right over the years is that their clergy live "on the patch", often the last professionals to still do so (though even if they do, they often live in enormous houses in comparison to the local housing stock). Here is a leader from church D describing exactly this, having returned to re-found a church there:

> Yeah that's it, we live on the estate. I don't think it matters too much where you come from, it's the fact that we actually live on the estate. I think it makes a massive difference because there's so many organizations that drive onto the estate, do their work and drive home again to their nice comfortable leafy house in the suburbs.

It may well have been that many of those in the churches we researched are not so aware of their location in the North. We didn't go looking for such data, but do know that just asking the questions we did probably made people more aware. We noted in the survey data that the churches we researched thought of themselves as mostly local and northern—they knew their location. However, what was interesting in relation to location were the stories of many of the leaders in the seven churches we visited

and how, most often, they were both insiders *and* outsiders to the places *leaders*
they were ministering in.

From the mid-nineteenth century there is a great deal of literature
about the development of *indigenous* leadership in nascent churches that
were created as part of the missionary movement outside of Europe in
that era. Even a century and more later, I was sent as a *mission partner,*
note the change of name, to work alongside colleagues in the Anglican
Church of Tanzania, and one of my tasks was the theological education
of local leadership in their language, Kiswahili. Henry Venn (1796–1873)
is well known for championing the "three-self" movement in the
indigenization of churches: self-governing, self-supporting and self-
propagating. Some people add a fourth self—self-theologizing, which is
synonymous with theological agency. To be "self-governing" a Church
body requires indigenous leadership at all levels, and this was the case
broadly for the Tanzanian Anglicans I joined and worked amongst in
the 1990s. It was interesting to me, however, to notice that there seemed
to be some kind of relationship between the most effective priests and
those who had married a life partner from outside their own tribe and
often spoke more than two languages (there are 120 different tribes with
distinct languages in Tanzania).

Thus, we need to complexify the idea of indigenous leadership, and
this is borne out by our research. It is hard to interrogate the data for
exact numbers, but a rough estimate shows that more than half, at the
very least, of those leaders (lay and ordained) in the churches we visited
had an experience like this from church G:

> I was born in Tynemouth, then spent early childhood in Pinner
> and teenage years in Scotland, in Dunblane, and then came back
> here to university. So, I was then back here for ten years, and then
> we went to the States for a short period, for about five years, then
> back to Woking, and then we came back here twenty years ago.
> And I kind of came as a result of prayer, didn't I? . . . And then
> both [name 1] and [name 2], who were the churchwardens were
> giving me a hug within a month, going, "You're a round peg in a
> round hole here, you know."

What makes connection?

Some had moved countries within the UK, had retained their original (often more Celtic) accent and this seemed to have helped their acceptance locally since they couldn't be as easily pigeonholed as southerners might be. Some had started in the North as in the example above, moved away and returned. Others had begun in the South and moved North and then made it "home", however long this had taken. What they all had in common was that they had crossed important internal (and sometimes external) cultural and linguistic boundaries in their lives. There were exceptions inevitably, though perhaps they prove the rule. A good example of such an exception would be a longstanding churchwarden (we won't say at which church in this case) who I met before and after the worship on the field visit (interestingly she had not been present at the leaders' focus group). Born and bred in the town, with her spouse she had run a small business for over thirty years and exhibited entrepreneurial and hard-working values. It was clear she acted as a bridge-person (even inter-cultural interpreter) between the "old" and the "new" elements in the growing congregation and she rejoiced in both the growth and her part in it.

It seems to us that this evidence confirms my hypothesis from Tanzania that where leaders have done personal inter-cultural work by changing their location, they can be more effective at enabling a local church to be connected across its own boundaries with the community around it (which we know has changed radically in its outlooks and beliefs in the last fifty to sixty years). It is interesting to read the stories of the location of Al Barrett and Ruth Harley (2020: 18–23) as they both crossed many boundaries of culture, class, gender and sexuality on their journey to where they are now. If we are right, and it would take another research project to look into the hypothesis, then this has serious implications for the training and development of so-called "indigenous" leadership, in places like the North, but also in general in places where the Church is under-represented.

In addition, while discussing indigeneity I would add something else I have noticed in the places I have been located throughout my working life, which is related to the research findings here. It has seemed to me that one of the longest journeys a leader can make is from a marginalized, impoverished community (whether in the UK or Tanzania) into learning skills, developing new capacity and gaining qualifications which usually take the person beyond it. Then to return to the place of origin (whether literally or somewhere like it) to serve alongside the people of that place, most often for much less financial reward than could be found elsewhere. We know it is hard for the "prophet to be accepted in their own country", but not all leaders are prophets and I have admired many individuals I have known who have taken this circular journey, as it costs them a great deal both on leaving and returning.

It is not part of Heaney's discussion of particularity, but the place of buildings in a post-colonial contextual theology is worth a mention as part of our discussion of location. Here we turn to Bickley (2018) who researches the relationship between local churches and what he calls "neighbourhood resilience" in the North East of England. The research demonstrates the importance of a) people (relationality and community, which we already know about at fuzzy boundaries), b) place (connecting exactly with the discussion here) and c) purpose, which he relates to positive spiritual capital, and which we will return to later.

In Chapter 2, we noted how, in different ways, all our research churches had intentionally engaged with their built environment— whether it had closed for good, been re-imagined and re-ordered, or needed to be utilized in a different way with the other buildings in the benefice. The best of these changes physically incorporated the fuzzy boundaries that were necessary for something to happen in relation to the community. The buildings thus transformed intentionally broke down the sacred/secular divide we inherit from modernity and the way our historic buildings contribute to the outward "flow" of the church which requires interrupting. In one case, at least, the rebuilding of a church and community centre went hand in hand with regeneration in the wider community, building a sense of hope in the future for everyone. Here is a literal, concrete example of how the past can become the compost of the future.

This is what Bickley calls "enacting the building" (2018: 73). It is not enough to own or have access to a building as a public community utility; it has to be connected relationally with the community in the myriad of ways we have seen possible in the research to be enacted. He points out that Christendom-legacy buildings can be a real burden and it is in fact a blessing when they burn or fall down! Once again compost comes to mind. This seeming disaster is a liberation into the post-colonial where the question "What might a neighbourhood need for the next hundred years, as opposed to the last?" can be answered positively.

There are other aspects of location which we have touched on in this book, but which we also have to admit are limits to the research. Our position as white, privileged and educated researchers biases our work in certain directions and were we to repeat the exercise in a longitudinal fashion this would no doubt need to be addressed more deeply.

Theological agency

Heaney states the question which faces Christians in the post-colony as: "Where is God in relation to empire/colonialism?" (2019: 44). It is the question in relation to the North of England that we have been raising since the development of *Northern Gospel, Northern Church* (2016). Many of us who contributed to that volume were born and bred in the North and others have adopted the North as home. A few of us would perhaps claim the title "theologian" in the formal trained and professional sense of that word, but none of us could claim much national and international reach for our theology. The only chapter in that book dedicated to an influential theologian, William Temple, by Stephen Spencer (2016: 109–122), offers a picture of someone educationally formed in the South until many of his ideas were forged by moving to the North (Manchester and York) in the second half of his life. I was trying to think of any published theologian I know who openly owns a Northernness and the only person I could think of is Anthony Reddie, the Black theologian who readily claims his roots in Bradford and the local brand of Methodism he grew up with there. I suspect it is highly significant that as a person of African-Caribbean descent Anthony knows and shares his location in the way he does—see his helpful method of doing this for ourselves in his book, *Is God Colour-blind?* (2009) which is quoted in full in *Being Interrupted* (2020: 16–18).

Our claim in this book is that by going to the fuzzy edge, or the margin as represented by the North in England, we can find God at work and clues to the future of churches in our nation. We noted the "gift" that these churches might be to the whole of the English Church in Chapter 3. I have written elsewhere about how God is found in the gaps, at the edge or in what is known as liminality (Carson, Fairhurst, Rooms & Withrow, 2021—see especially Chapter 12). This is also true at both the local, church level and at the regional.

I spend a lot of my time, when not researching, helping local churches to change their deep culture and behaviours with a three-year process called *Partnership for Missional Church*.[10] As well as enabling them to become fuzzy at their edges we also attempt to liberate their members from the prison of not being able to speak about God in public. Another of the effects of modernity on the church is to turn its members into "practical atheists". That is, when asked to talk about what God is up to we do not, in general, begin the response with God as the subject of an active verb. When sharing these ideas with local churches, we often say that if the government passed a law banning talking about God, we would all start doing it, but they haven't and we don't. We have voluntarily imprisoned ourselves in the cage of modernity, giving in to the privatization of religion where it remains safely tucked away in our hearts. What is evident from this research is that the people we met, both leaders and new converts, had a language and a set of behaviours that bucked this trend. They had, to employ Heaney's language, *theological agency*—permission to name what God was up to in their individual and collective lives. And to go further we noted the new Christians also had agency *per se* in their faith and action: they had a place and permission to be their best selves in the Christian community they were joining.

It is hard sometimes to persuade people of the reality of practical atheism, since of course we all believe, cognitively, in God. Yet the evidence is overwhelming from data we collect from churches that have engaged with the change process we are utilizing. We suggest here is another opportunity for composting. There is a relinquishing (Barrett & Harley, 2020: 175) and even a repentance (2020: 179) that is required so that we can take up our theological agency in new, receptive and

---

[10] <https://churchmissionsociety.org/churches/partnership-missional-church/>, accessed 29 December 2020.

appropriate ways. Indeed, there is a needful conversion here, which takes us to Heaney's engagement with coloniality through developing critical awareness.

Coloniality

We have already noted how the first response to be made to the coloniality the North experiences is that of becoming critically aware by making the invisible visible: that is, "identifying and naming those that have been made invisible" (Heaney, 2018: 76). The research and its presentation in this book are testament to the amazing, but often hidden people we met on our travels who are composting for new life across the North.

Going beyond our human responses to coloniality Heaney also suggests we should be intentionally making "the invisible God visible in the circumstances of coloniality" (2018: 78). We have been working on the assumption that God is at work in the North of England even where, seemingly, the church-as-it-was is dying. Is it possible then to notice the activity of God in what has been happening in these last decades in the North? We'll say more about how we see God at work in our research churches in the next chapter, but for now let's ask that bigger question about God and the end of Christendom.

Elaine Heath is a Methodist minister and scholar of mission and evangelism based in the eastern United States. Consistently over the last few years, starting with her important book on evangelism (2017), she has been calling the Church to follow Jesus faithfully in discipleship. For Elaine this means embracing the same shape of life that Jesus did which is outlined by St Paul in Philippians 2:5–11. In verse 5, the NRSV has "let the same mind be in you that was in Christ Jesus". The word "mind" in this verse is not just our brains! It describes a wisdom, a kind of knowing that arises from acting in our bodies and learning from that action—embodied knowing and practical wisdom (Rooms, 2012). In the following verses we have the whole movement of Christ from heaven to earth and back again which St Paul is exhorting us to imitate in an embodied fashion. Elaine extrapolates a little between verses 8 and 9 from other places in the Bible and the creeds which describe what happens to

Jesus between his death and resurrection—so she concludes *the Church has to follow Jesus to hell* (cf. 1 Peter 3:19).[11] When I first heard her say this there was a shocked silence in the room (and in myself, I must admit), but it seems some of the experiences we heard about on our travels were pretty "hellish". Others speak of the importance of staying with the dead Christ on Holy Saturday as a way of learning relinquishment, powerlessness and the chance to become compost (e.g. Barrett & Harley, 2020: 191, 200).

If this is the shape of discipleship that God in Christ himself has chosen then might we not be able to discern God's activity in the death of Christendom? Perhaps we might even say tentatively that God wills it, just as it seems the Israelites were taken into exile within the purposes of God, as described in the Hebrew Bible. It is perhaps too easily done, but it is popular to speak of how the Church in this country is constantly "re-arranging the deckchairs on the Titanic" as a metaphor for the almost permanent re-organization of parish, circuit and regional church boundaries that goes on as a response to the slow decline of the Church, especially the numbers of available clergy. In this metaphor then we are hypothesizing that God might be the iceberg, or at the very least wills it to be there for the Church to founder on. Another shocking thought, perhaps. There is, no doubt, much more to be said here, but it will need to wait until we have a chance to go deeper (under the surface of the iceberg?) in the further book we plan to write.

Hybridization

Heaney defines hybridization like this: "a strategy employed toward decolonization that subverts the power of colonial authority and culture by mixing it with, for example, cultural practices, language, philosophy, and texts from the colonized culture" (2019: 5). Again, we'll need to take this agenda further and deeper in the next book, but for now we can

---

[11]   The reader can watch Elaine Heath speak about this at <https://www.theworkofthepeople.com/go-to-hell>, though there is a donation wall part way through, accessed 7 January 2021.

demonstrate aspects of this effect at work in the churches we visited, particularly in some features of their worship. While not all the mixing is taking place with "texts from the colonized culture", what seems to be happening is a re-imagining of worship towards what, sometimes pragmatically, "works" in the local culture and context and in relation to the fuzzy boundaries of the church which allow different sorts of people from the locality to participate.

We also claim, therefore, that hybridization gives another meaning or aspect to our title of "Fuzzy Church", since the worship practices we came across blurred boundaries between traditional (Christendom) denominational practices and borrowed others from many and varied sources.

So, what's different about worship in these places that makes it "hybrid"? First it doesn't just happen on a Sunday, or even in some places ever on a Sunday! In fact, it is more a demonstration that Christian life and worship can be enacted anytime and anywhere throughout the week. Communion can be "tacked on" to a lunch club, but changes the whole nature of the hospitality that happens there. Traditional, what might be thought of as "Catholic" practices, such as the lighting of candles, are available alongside (almost everywhere) a version of Pentecostal "testimony" which sometimes gets mixed up in the notices. Prayer for healing in various guises is possible. There are connections made between the local and the global, in the use of different languages and in the borrowing of Christian comedy culture from the United States in one place. Some leaders worry whether the church hierarchy will really approve of such fuzziness, but it seems they do. It is also clear to us that, most likely, even if they didn't like it the local leaders would not change much.

how far autonomy?

This brings us to another post-colonial tactic worth discussing here—that of *mimicry* (Heaney, 2019: 4). While some forms of mimicry can be simply the aping of the more powerful culture so as to "fit in", mimicry can also be "directly subversive". I am reminded of a story from Tanzania when so-called "ethical tourism" was becoming popular in the time I was there. One of the experiences the tourists were exposed to was a "traditional" Maasai Moran (young men) dance on the basis, presumably, that everyone loves a good song and dance act. Such things cross cultures

(q.v Girard ?)

fairly easily. The men stand in a line in the traditional dress of a wrap-around red blanket and staff. The dance consists of singing and jumping up and down on the spot to the beat of the song, not unlike what was called "pogoing" in the heyday of punk rock music. It all looked very traditional except that the song, when translated, went something like "Leave us alone you **!!#&%$ tourists and give us your money!" Heaney tells a not dissimilar story from Ireland (2019: 5).

There is no doubt that some of the churches we researched were most likely still complicit in many kinds of colonialism. Yet they were often, at the same time, subverting the "givenness" of secularization and the death of the church in their communities and subverting traditional ways of being the church by becoming fuzzy on the inside and the outside. We touched on the importance of irony in Chapter 2 in relation to humour and there is something deeply ironic about the way the dying of one thing can provide compost for another. Which takes us neatly to the final one of Heaney's characteristics of post-colonial contextual theology—that of resistance.

Resistance

We already reached a conclusion about resistance in Chapter 2 and noted how in relation to the reign of God which is characterized by *shalom* (Heaney, 2019: 132) resistance is part of the good news, the gospel. Resistance, Heaney tells us, is at root about telling a different story (2019: 126) and once again this is what we have been attempting in our research. Resistance is not always about setting ourselves over against the other, though that is sometimes necessary. It perhaps connects suggestively via *shalom*, based on human relationality, with Barrett and Harley's use of the term "respiring" (2020: 214). Respiration is another organic term for what plants do at night and is related metaphorically to the recovery of hope, courage and strength. Barrett and Harley also connect it to the way Jesus breathes on the dispirited disciples in the locked room in John 20:21–2. I suspect there is quite a lot of respiration going on in a compost heap.

Bickley (2018) is also interested in the re-telling of story in relation to resistance but adds a note of caution. Some stories that are told can be resistant, but when arising in a marginal context can also easily trap their tellers in a narrative of decline. We too have noted this tendency even as we have been doing the work of raising the theological profile of the North (a hardening of the northern chip on the shoulder occurs, it seems). Such stories can become solely "if only" stories rather than the "what if" stories that lead to what Bickley is searching for in marginal northern communities: *resilience* (2018: 85). *What if* northern churches where something is happening are the clue to the future of the English, if not Western Church? *What if* "fuzzy" church, discovered in the North, became the watchword for how church can be alive and flourishing? *What if* the decomposing northern Church is the soil in which there is resurrection for Christians in a post-colonial world?

Bickley is clear that telling a different story around "what if" builds what he calls spiritual capital, defined as a "stockpile of hope, activism and purpose" (2018: 90). This could be a description of our research churches. They had stockpiles of hope, activism and purpose, and the combination of all three means, we think, that they are less likely to burn out. Without purpose and hope, activism becomes disparate, dissipated and de-energizing. Without hope and activism, purpose is just a bunch of nice-to-have goals. Without activism and purpose, hope turns easily into pie-in-the-sky.

A contextual northern theology which deals with life in the post-colony will therefore engage spiritual capital "which draws attention to the importance of non-tangible factors of identity, culture and expectation" (2018: 96). In other words, despite these factors being difficult to measure empirically it is vital to pay attention to them. And we know (and have noted elsewhere in the book) that spiritual capital creates relational capital at the fuzzy boundary of Church and world. In turn, relational capital creates sustainable economic capital in a cascade which normally flows in that direction. It is much harder to make it flow in the other direction, which is why throwing money at churches, dioceses and districts rarely works. The best historical illustration of this cascade I can think of is German city centre churches which often have small shops embedded in the outer walls of the church (have a look at pictures of the Church of the Holy Spirit in Heidelberg—I don't know if it happens elsewhere in Europe, or is a peculiar Lutheran phenomenon). The spiritual capital on display in the building creates economic capital from the relational capital of those who come to experience the spiritual capital. It is no surprise that the shops are at the very boundary of the church building and its context. The closest we have to this would be St Martin-in-the-Fields in Trafalgar Square, which pays particular attention to its fuzzy boundary with the four "C"s of its growing *HeartEdge Network*: Congregation, Culture, Commerce and Compassion.[12]

We have presented, therefore, in this chapter what we claim is a "nuanced post-colonial contextual theology from the North of England". We know, however, that it is only a start, the bare bones, and there is much more that can be said, and we hope to do that in our second book. For the moment, we are clear that there is a future and a hope for the gospel in the North of England, arising out of intentional compost-making from the debris of Christendom, and we look in our final chapter in more detail at how God is at work there.

Questions for reflection

1. What is the story of your "location" and where you find yourself now? How much of an insider or an outsider are you to the community or communities you find yourself living and working in? What difference does being an insider/outsider or a mixture make?

2. What do you think about the idea that church has to "go to hell", to embrace composting in our current time for her to find new life? What might this look like for your Christian community?

3. What "hybridization" do you notice going on in your church's worship? Where have you borrowed from? If there is such mixing what is it that the different "borrowings" contribute to the whole?

4. What's the story that your church tells about itself, and how might it become more of a *"what if"* story?

---

[12] <https://www.heartedge.org/about-us/about-us>, accessed 8 January 2021.

CHAPTER 7

Joining in the dance

In this final chapter, and true to the nature of practical theology (and good sermons), we're going back to the beginning of our book and returning to the question of how we join in with God's mission within our communities. And in doing so, I hope we can answer a question that may have arisen in your mind as you've been reading about how God is at work in the North of England: why is this all so difficult? Why are the things that are happening a bit—well—small, embryonic? Why does such "success" as we have discerned seem so fragile? And there's a question that perhaps lies behind this: if God is loving and powerful, why doesn't God make our churches stronger, bigger, better, more effective? If God wants the same things that we want—people discovering faith, new Christian community being formed, context and culture impacted and transformed—why don't we see more of this? Why is this all so tough? In this chapter, I want to dig down into some of those questions and look at how God is bringing about change in the North of England, and the nature of the power that God uses to do that.

Joining in with God's mission

Back in Chapter 1, we described God's mission in the world, the *missio Dei*. We mentioned Bevans and Schroeder's description of God as being like a dance which we are invited to join in with. Bevans and Schroeder write that God doesn't have a mission—God is mission!—and they invite us to join in with "that great Conga Line that has moved through the world since the beginning of time and that is also the heartbeat of God's deepest self" (Bevans & Schroeder, 2011: 17).

When Bevans and Schroeder put it like that, I can't resist wanting to join in that dance. But how do we actually do this? If you're like me, you'd struggle to know the steps. Half of my family are dancers: my aunt ran a dance school at one point, and my sister and cousin have been professional dancers. I was asked to leave a ballet class at the age of four, because I insisted on dancing my own steps. Although I watch *Strictly Come Dancing* each year and imagine myself to be an expert on the Charleston, if my sister invited me to actually dance, I wouldn't know where to start. I'd probably even struggle with Bevans and Schroeder's conga line. And joining in with God's mission in our local communities can feel similarly daunting.

The first step we need to take is to discern where God is already at work. If we remember that the mission is God's, not ours, we are joining in with something that's already happening, not creating something from scratch. So, our first step is to spot where God is at work in our local area, where God is already changing things. That's what we've been doing in this book: paying careful attention to the North of England, trying to spot the ways that God is changing lives and communities. We've been engaged in a careful process of discernment of God's mission in the North.   *dishl diagnosis'?*

Discernment

Another author who we mentioned in Chapter 1 was Tim Gorringe, when we agreed with his definition of culture as the process by which God makes us and keeps people human (Gorringe, 2004: 4). He's also got some interesting arguments when it comes to the question of how we discern God at work in the world. In *Discerning Spirit: A Theology of Revelation*, Gorringe argues that discernment is all about learning to pay attention to the Holy Spirit (Gorringe, 1990: 2). For Gorringe, there are two elements of discernment and pneumatology (the study of the Holy Spirit): God the "Wholly Other", strange, and beyond human experience, and God active and encountered in human experience (Gorringe, 1990: 6). Gorringe argues that revelation is the spark between these two poles, and that to know more about the Spirit we must wrestle with discernment in this paradox. He argues that to find the criterion for discernment of God, we must look for a "Christic structure", or in our words, something that looks like or is at least comparable to how Christ would have things be. Quoting Leonardo Boff, Gorringe argues that every time someone opens to God and the other, wherever people seek justice, reconciliation and forgiveness, a Christic structure and true Christianity can be found (Gorringe, 1990: 46). Christ must always be found "outside the camp", and it is in these places where the Spirit blows (Gorringe, 1990: 136).

This is the attitude we found in our fuzzy churches: they were open to being changed by the "others" who brought challenge and difference, as well as encountering God through their own experiences. They sought Christ outside their normal services and structures and found him there. I am reminded of the luncheon club for lonely older men in church G: the church went outside their normal pattern of Sunday services to put on the club and were shown that Christ was already there. The men who met wanted communion with Christ, not just a soup lunch. The "spark" that shows the Spirit at work was there, a little flash of light connecting with the light already in those men, joining them together and making a much brighter light out of the whole as they formed a community of Christ.

And Gorringe is clear that community is a crucial element in this encounter with God and the other. For Gorringe, community is at the heart of the nature of God: he argues that the Triune God is community, and it is only in community that we encounter God. As we relate to other people, we are in the image of God, "for the image is the echoing of the relationship God is. As, and only as, we relate we live in the Spirit" (1990: 74). Community is also the only place of the revelation of God: "The one who is other to me, who I cannot ultimately colonize, who resists me and interrogates and so stands outside my totality is always the potential place of revelation—what I cannot tell myself." Gorringe recognizes that this concept is difficult for many in the West, with a focus on the individual and not the community, but argues that individualism has no place in the Old or New Testament. Gorringe does not argue that community is inherently a place of grace: it can also be a channel for destruction, where community solidarity is pitted against communal solidarity (Gorringe, 1990: 79). Nevertheless, community can be "'sacramental' . . . a means or a channel of 'grace', a mediator of the forgiving, healing, restorative power of God" (Gorringe, 1990: 79).

Again, this has great resonance with the northern churches we studied, for whom community was a vital part of the gospel and their surrounding culture. Our churches were radically welcoming, prepared to be disrupted and interrupted to engage people in community building. In the church, new Christians found deep communion with other people. And our churches weren't afraid to have fuzzy boundaries between the church community and the people outside the church. We discerned the Spirit at work in the communities of these churches.

pneumatology
= crucial

This also raises the question of in whom the Holy Spirit lives, or resides, or is. This is an area of thought which will divide people: does the Holy Spirit reside only in people who are Christians, or is the Holy Spirit present and active in all people? Christians who agree with the former view would perhaps look to Acts 2, seeing the Holy Spirit descending on the apostles, not the whole of the crowd (though there is other evidence to the contrary later in the book in, for instance, the openness of Cornelius and Lydia). Christians who understand the Holy Spirit as residing in all people are more likely to look to Creation, and see God creating humans in the image of God as including the indwelling of the Holy Spirit. It is the latter view which makes sense of the *missio Dei*, the idea that God is already at work in people's lives, and we are invited to join in. When we evangelize, we aren't taking an unknown God to people, we are helping people recognize how God has already been at work in their lives through the person of the Holy Spirit. Now, it may be that the Holy Spirit is more active in people's lives, more able to give people gifts, when people are aware of who that Spirit is: the Spirit of God, of Jesus Christ. But if we understand God to be at work in people's lives, we must acknowledge that the Holy Spirit is not just a person who resides in and works in the lives of Christians, but all people who were created by a loving God.

Kirsteen Kim also gives us some markers on how to discern God at work in people's lives, in our communities outside the church. In her 2012 book on pneumatology and world mission, *Joining in with the Spirit*, she argues that the Holy Spirit can only be encountered through human culture, as the gospel is never encountered and the Holy Spirit never at work except within a particular cultural setting (Kim, 2012: 42). By now you'll have realized we like her approach here! She gives us some ways in which we can discern if the Holy Spirit is at work in our communities:

> The criterion for Christian discernment is clear; the Holy Spirit is the Spirit of Jesus Christ. The Holy Spirit is not present only where there is explicit Christian confession but where there is a likeness of Christ. This likeness may be in character or characteristics, the "love, joy, peace, patience, kindness, generosity, faithfulness, gentleness, and self-control" which are the fruit of the Spirit (Gal. 5:22–3; cf. Rom. 12:9–21). Or it may be in action or activity, where the gifts of the Spirit are being exercised in love for the building up of the body (1 Cor. 12–14) and where people are being liberated, healed, helped, forgiven and reconciled (e.g. Luke 4:18–19; John 20:21–3; Rom. 8:22–6).
>
> These are the marks of the Spirit of God shown in Jesus Christ. This Christ-likeness is what we look for when we identify where the Spirit is at work in order to join in God's mission (Kim, 2012: 36).

So, if we're trying to discern God at work in our communities in order to join in with God's dance of mission, we firstly need to pay close attention to the places where the spark of God, the "Wholly Other" meets God active and encountered in human experience (Gorringe, 1990: 6). It will remind us of the works of Jesus, and look like justice, reconciliation and forgiveness. We will see love, joy, peace, patience, kindness, generosity, faithfulness, gentleness and self-control, and people being liberated, healed, helped, forgiven and reconciled.

How God makes things happen

At the beginning of this chapter, I asked the question: why is this all so difficult? Why doesn't God use God's power to bring about true flourishing in our churches and the communities they serve? The answer to some of that question lies in the way God seems to be using power in the North of England today. I hope this exploration will help us be more attuned to God's mission, and more able to discern the work of the Holy Spirit. And it involves diving deeper into a few of the ways Kirsteen Kim says we can spot the presence of the Holy Spirit: patience, kindness and gentleness.

In Chapter 2, Nigel looked at Karl Spracklen's definitions of Northernness. Spracklen argues that Northernness is essentially a "made up" thing constructed from "various myths and invented traditions": a simulacrum, something which has no origin or truth behind it at all. Spracklen explained the paradox of the reality of Northernness by comparing it to sympathetic magic:

> Northernness is a form of sympathetic magic, which northerners choose to perform, albeit through the constraints of hegemonic cultural formations and the symbolic boundaries and invented traditions of imagined community (Spracklen, 2016: 14).

Nigel pointed out that Spracklen's understanding of Northernness as sympathetic magic feels rather sad, as there can be no change, no transformation from the current situation.

As Christians, deep in the DNA of our faith is the understanding that God can and does change the world (though we often differ about *how* God does that). Nigel and I profoundly disagree with Spracklen that Northernness is something that has to be performed to maintain the status quo of identity and community. We believe that God has made the North of England and sees that it is good. But God also sees that people's lives have been hurt by poverty and deprivation, by a lack of care and attention from those who govern and do business with the North. Our book has been an attempt to show what God is doing in changing people's lives, giving them hope for something better, and a spirit of community to change others' lives too. Unlike the idea of sympathetic magic, God can enact real change. God has power to change the status quo, and by understanding what that power looks like, we can be more attuned to where it is happening, and where we need to be joining in.

When we see God's power at work through the Spirit, changing situations in our local communities, we will see something that is patient, kind and gentle. We can sometimes assume that, if God is all-powerful,

power

we will see the full force of that power in our world today. And in our world of inequality, we can even see power as a negative thing. Andy Crouch draws this out in his book *Playing God: Redeeming the Gift of Power* when he recalls a conversation with a university professor who instinctively saw power as a damaging thing that had to be contained and limited, without perhaps recognizing the positive power that she wielded in her role (Crouch, 2013: 9). And I wonder if it is particularly complicated for Christians, since when we think about power, we're not just thinking about it in a human sense, but also a divine one. As reflective Christians living in our world today, we can see the evil that can be wielded by people and organizations in power, but also recognize the good of the power of God. Is it simply the case that power is good or bad depending on who is using it, or are there other factors at stake?

This is something that a group of Birmingham Christians wrestled with in the 1980s and is described by Laurie Green in *Power to the Powerless*. Green describes how, as the parish of St Chad's Erdington engaged in "theology brought to life", they explored the nature of power. They identified five types of power: physical, political, economic, cultural and spiritual, and tentatively gave a definition of power as "the ability to change the direction of something" (Green, 1987: 92–99). Wrestling with the powerlessness of the people in their Birmingham community, they identified that power misused by individuals was bad enough, but power became exponentially worse when it was held by faceless structures. They talked about how individual doctors, nurses or administrators might want to help someone who was ill, but the healthcare system meant that people sometimes had to suffer for years before they could be treated (Green, 1987: 100). Turning to scripture, they reflected on structures that held power, both in their own community and in scripture. They studied Paul's letter to the Colossians and, looking at Colossians 1:16–17, came to the view that although the "systems or structures are held together through and for Christ as honourable creations at his service", they can be corrupted. One of Green's theology group, Ray, put it like this:

> The thing is ... we've sorted out that these structures are
> very powerful and that they're good to have—given by God, I
> suppose—but we've said earlier that when evil and sin gets into

power

them they can be worse than really bad individuals. It's all very well Paul saying they're good to start with, but we know they can end up pretty bad. It rather reminds me of the Book of Genesis where things begin perfectly in the Garden of Eden but then everything goes wrong (Green, 1987: 102).

Andy Crouch makes a similar point from an American perspective in *Playing God* that institutions can become corrupted by power and can even become like zombies: full of deadly power "that brings no flourishing, is mute and inert, yet threatens to consume all life and love" (Crouch, 2013: 197). He discusses the idea that the greatest difference between white evangelical Protestants and black Protestants in the USA is not their theology or their desire for racial reconciliation, but the white evangelicals' lack of understanding of corrupt institutions:

> When evangelicals think about solving social problems like the legacy of slavery and racism in the United States, they think almost exclusively in terms of personal, one-on-one relationships— which is why so many white evangelicals can imagine the problem of racism is solved if they simply have a handful of friends of other races ... Black Christians instinctively know that for the gospel to keep transforming America's sorry racial story, it will have to keep challenging these deeply ingrained patterns and the structures that even now perpetuate them (Crouch, 2013: 201).

In the European mind, if we think of the ultimate corruption of power, there's a good chance we'll think of the Nazis. Hannah Arendt was a German/American political theorist, born in 1906 to a Jewish family; she experienced persecution under the Nazis in 1930s Germany for conducting research into the Nazis' anti-Semitism. She fled to the USA in the 1940s and is best known for her book examining the trial of Adolf Eichmann. Arendt studied the evil of the Nazis and coined the phrase "the banality of evil" to describe how Eichmann and other Nazis committed horrifying acts of cruelty by "just doing their jobs": there are perhaps parallels here with Crouch's idea of zombie organizations. In her 1970 book *On Violence*, Arendt explored the relationship between violence,

power

war and power in the twentieth century. She argued that, although there are strong links between violence and power, they are not the same thing. She saw violence as something that acts in the name of something else, but power as an end in itself:

> Power is indeed the essence of all government, but violence is not. Violence is by nature instrumental; like all means, it always stands in need of guidance and justification through the end it pursues. And what needs justification by something else cannot be the essence of anything. The end of war—end taken in its twofold meaning—is peace or victory; but to the question "And what is the end of peace?" there is no answer. Peace is an absolute . . . Power is in the same category; it is, as they say, "an end in itself" (Arendt, 1970: 51).

The British political theorist Steven Lukes made a similar argument to Arendt. He wrote that power is not always a negative, oppressive category: "You can be powerful by satisfying and advancing others' interests . . . power as domination is only one species of power" (Lukes, 2004: 12). Power is a potentiality, not an actuality, and it is not always actualized. Taking the writings of the Dutch philosopher Spinoza, Lukes argues that power exhibits two distinct variants: *potentia* and *potestas* (Lukes, 2004: 73). *Potentia* is the power of things in nature, including humans, to exist and act, whereas *potestas* is being in the power of another. "Power as *potestas*, or 'power over', is, therefore, a sub-concept of power as *potentia*: it is the ability to have another or others in your power, by constraining their choices, thereby securing their compliance" (Lukes, 2004: 73).

Lukes' breakdown of power into *potentia* and *potestas* is really useful when we are looking at the power of God. We can describe God's power as being an absolute category, an end in itself. God is all-powerful. And this sense of power as *potestas* is what we see being abused and zombified in faceless organizations, in racist institutions, in Nazi Germany. We discussed colonialism and coloniality in the last chapter: colonialism is *potestas* in action, power over other people. But God's power as we see it in our world today has more of the sense of *potentia*, the power of existing and acting. God actively gives up the sense of *potestas* and does not use power to dominate others. We see this most clearly in the person of Jesus.

It was Jesus who transformed the thinking of Laurie Green's Birmingham theology group when it came to power. In studying Jesus' birth, death and resurrection, they saw how power can be exercised without domination. They saw Jesus' obedience to death on the cross as total solidarity with people who are oppressed by evil, displaying evil's ugliness to the world, God's ultimate protest against evil, and the key to unlocking history (Green, 1987: 119). They understood that Jesus' death was also the first fruits of a restored humanity, returning the evil of corrupted power structures back in their correct place, behind Jesus, and restoring the good order of God's creation. Green describes it like this:

> Our recent learning had taught us to discern that a perversion occurs when, instead of these [humanly created] structures remaining necessary tools in the struggle, they take on a dominating life of their own . . . When Jesus confronts evil on the cross, in doing so he has restored creation at its heart and the structures are put back into perspective so we can now demand that they are put in a subservient relationship to humanity. If we ever see them attempting to usurp the place of God or humanity we are now at liberty to engage them and renounce them fearlessly (1987: 121).

Green and his theology group identified that it is part of God's nature not to dominate (we might say not to exercise *potestas*), writing:

> Within this framework [of the cross and resurrection] Jesus has now also given us a proper appreciation of God's nature as He who will not dominate. Our group project had taught us time and again that the underlying evil in human experience derives from precisely this yearning in individuals and in the structures to dominate and use power for their own ends . . . And it was against this tendency that Jesus strove and won (1987: 122).

The idea of God as "The One who will not dominate" also comes through
in the work of the Swiss biblical scholar Hans-Ruedi Weber. In *Power:
Focus for a Biblical Theology*, Weber conducted a thorough survey of the
theme of power as it occurs in the Bible. Weber identified six "trajectories
of faith" in relation to power that emerge from the scriptures: the liberating
acts of God, the royal rulers who govern Israel under God's power, the
power of God's enlightening wisdom, the power of God's holy presence,
God's vindication of the poor, and God's judgment and re-creation of
a new heaven and a new earth (Weber, 1989: 22–3). While Weber is
careful to articulate that there is no short or simple answer to the question
"what does the Bible say about power?", he does describe how all his six
trajectories of faith "converge on the life, death and resurrection of Jesus
Christ", where the notion of power is turned upside down:

> Meeting this Jesus of Nazareth and following his way becomes
> particularly upsetting in the midst of today's power struggles.
> He turns upside down our thinking, attitudes and actions, as
> those readers experience who attempt to draw out the lines
> and consequences from the biblical testimonies to their own
> involvement in the struggles for justice, peace and safeguarding
> of creation in today's world. With a variety of emphases all New
> Testament witnesses testify that Jesus made a total abdication of
> power as power is traditionally understood. He did so in order to
> endow us with a new kind of power. Summing up in one sentence
> one might say: Jesus transforms the love of power into the power
> of love (Weber, 1989: 166–7).

So, if we understand that God is "The One who will not dominate", who
turns "the love of power into the power of love" through the person
of Jesus, we cannot expect the Holy Spirit to act with *potestas* in our
world today, forcing economic and social transformation, or packed-out
churches. The identifying marks of the Spirit at work will be patience,
kindness and gentleness, not domination or force. And yet, that can
sometimes feel frustrating.

Cracks in the pavement

In this chapter, I've argued that if we want to join in with God's mission in our communities, we need to learn to listen to where the Holy Spirit is already at work in our context and culture. We need to pay attention to places where new growth is happening, where we see acts of love, joy, peace, patience, kindness, gentleness and self-control, and where people are being liberated, healed, helped, forgiven and reconciled (Kim, 2012: 36). We've explored that these acts reflect the gentle, patient and kind nature of God, and how God chooses to use power in the world today. *McQuarrie*? We've looked at God as "The One who does not dominate", but instead is the one who gives up the love of power for the power of love.

I now want to tie this into something Nigel described in the last chapter: how our declining church institutions can make wonderful compost for the new growth of the Spirit in the North of England. In Chapter 3, we explored the idea of Christendom (when the Christian Church is a dominant religious, political and social power in a country) and post-Christendom (when the Christian Church has become distanced from the population and lost its political and societal power). We acknowledged that although we no longer live in a time of Christendom in the UK, it can be hard to let go of the sense that the Church should still be a dominant power in a country. And as well as being in a post-Christendom situation, we discussed in Chapter 6 how the North of England can be seen as being in a post-colonial situation. If the North has historically been subjugated by the political powers in the South, it is now in a position of coloniality and resistance.

And in that place, between the new shoots of Spirit-filled life and the stony (or, perhaps better, concrete) context, is where our churches find themselves. Above, I mentioned how Laurie Green's theology group discovered that when institutions were corrupted by power, they could be even worse than powerful people. Andy Crouch also asserted that institutions can become corrupted by power, and can even become like zombies, full of deadly power "that brings no flourishing, is mute and inert, yet threatens to consume all life and love" (Crouch, 2013: 197). I think there is a very real argument to be made that the established Church in England has had times when it came close to this state, bound up in its own importance and dominating the people it was meant to serve. In our own day and age, it is something we need to continually check about our own churches. If we love the God who gave up power, are there ways we need to give up power in our own country and communities?

In Stephen Sykes' book *Power and Christian Theology*, Sykes introduces us to the relationship between sacrifice and power, arguing that sacrifice is the key concept that defines how Christians should live in relationship to power (Sykes, 2006: 116). He warns us that the concept of sacrifice does not resolve the ambivalence of power, its potential for good and for bad, and that the idea of sacrifice can itself be hijacked by those wanting to abuse power for their own gain. However, the concept of sacrifice helps explain how God approaches power in the person of Jesus Christ (Sykes, 2006: 117). Sykes' book on power is a good read for anyone wanting to think about this concept in further depth, as is Andy Crouch's *Playing God: Redeeming the Gift of Power*. As a way of addressing the relationship between the Church, power and sacrifice, Crouch encourages us to think about the "trustees" of institutions and organizations (Crouch, 2013: 216). When he talks about trustees, he's not referring to a board of trustees in a formal or legal sense, but those who can be trusted to lead. And one of the criteria he uses to discern whether people can be these leaders, these trustees, is if they have forgiven the institution they are being asked to lead. Crouch encourages us to appoint as trustees people who have been at the sharp end of injustice, and who can be trusted to weed it out in the future. He puts it like this:

> They are not trustees who pretend that their institutions somehow escape the idolatry and injustice that shadow even the noblest human efforts, but neither are they trustees who have seen the dark truth about their own institutions and cynically refused to extend mercy and hope. Trustees have seen, and borne, the worst that institutions can do—and yet they have somehow escaped the abyss of cynicism. Instead they enter into the life of their institutions, embodying a better way, bearing the institution's pain and offering hope (Crouch, 2013: 216).

This feels like a huge ask, for both institutions and potential trustees! If you had been hurt and treated badly by an institution, would you want to have anything to do with it in the future, let alone forgive it? When I think about organizations that have hurt me, I know that I feel cynical about them: could I allow myself to extend mercy to them and get involved in their life again? It feels pretty tough.

It's also hard for institutions, including churches, to invite people that they have hurt to become leaders within them. It means acknowledging injustice and wrongdoing. The Church of England is starting to acknowledge the recent history of institutional racism in the Church (see General Synod's apology for racism since the Windrush generation in February, 2020): can it now ask more Black and minority ethnic people to be the Church's trustees? This second step means that white people— bishops, clergy and lay people—will need to lay down or sacrifice their own positions of power and influence in the Church, for other people to pick these up. παραδιδωμι

When it comes to our own churches, can we look at who's on the PCC, who gets to speak in our services, who decides what activities our church gets involved in? Do the people making these decisions look like the wider community they serve? Are they people who might have been previously overlooked by the church, whether that's because of their colour, or their class, their gender or sexuality? Can we allow the usual decision-making structures of church to be interrupted by the other, and make the boundaries of these structures more porous? Looking at who makes the decisions in our churches and at where we need to give up power isn't just to ensure the health of our own churches, but to join in the places where God seems to be at work. In church C, the person who was leading at the time of our visit was working out how people recovering from addiction could become leaders too. In church E, the middle-class leadership deliberately encouraged local people to become churchwardens and PCC members, encouraging them despite their lack of confidence in themselves. This was the church where, during our visit, much of the notices slot was filled by people who couldn't speak English, sharing their testimonies of how God had been at work in their lives. The people from beyond the normal boundaries had been invited in to become the trustees of the church.

So yes, it's hard to relinquish or sacrifice power. And it is hard for people the church has harmed or overlooked to become trustees of that church. But it can happen, with gentleness, kindness and patience. It's a reconciliation of relationships and the restoration of the image of God at the heart of our churches. And it can happen despite, perhaps because of, the death of Christendom in the UK. We really shouldn't be surprised at this: deep in the heart of our faith, in the heart of God, is resurrection. Jesus knew death, just as our communities in the North of England know death. But Jesus also knew the Spirit-filled life of resurrection, and if we live our Christian lives to the pattern of Jesus, we will know that resurrection too. If our church institutions die, we have seen that their remains can potentially make amazing compost for the Spirit to grow new life! The resurrected bodies of these churches will look a bit different, with fuzzy insides and edges and lots of different people leading together, but we have nothing to fear. We can join in with what Brueggemann describes as an "intense practice of hope" (Brueggemann, 1997: 106), and participate in that resurrection life.

Final thoughts?

As we join in with what God is up to, and join in with God at work in our communities, we will be aware of how difficult the task seems to be. It's easy to wish that God would miraculously force huge changes on our world to bring it in line with God's desires, and to bring about the kingdom of God. But in our research with churches in the North, that is not how we've seen God at work. We have discovered that God works with kindness, gentleness and patience, that the gospel in the North has the sound of freedom and fragility, of authenticity, community and humour. The power of the Spirit at work could perhaps be described as new life coming through death and deprivation, like new shoots pushing up through cracks in the pavement.

At this point, you may be feeling that gentleness, kindness and patience don't seem particularly powerful. You may even feel that these concepts are a bit fluffy, a bit "nice", or even frivolous. They don't seem particularly tough, robust or even resilient. But to join in with God

working in gentleness, kindness and patience requires extraordinary
toughness and discipline. It means carrying on even when things are
harsh and barren, when you don't seem to make any progress. Staying
in ministry in the hardest places in the North means you need to put in
the hard yards. When we talk about churches where God is at work as
being "fuzzy", this doesn't mean they're soft! If churches stand with God
and their communities, being true to God and open to change, they will
find this to be very hard work. It takes strength, the willingness to have
tough discussions and to disappoint some people within the church. It
takes discipline to stay the course, and not retreat into being a cosy sort
of club when things get rough. But God is there, with more than enough
patience, gentleness and kindness to spare.

So, we're back at the beginning again, thinking how we can join in
with God's mission. We've been in a circle, or perhaps a spiral: now we've
learned something about how God is at work in the North of England,
is this a new beginning? Can we put this learning into practice in our
own communities? Do you want to compare our findings with how
you see God at work in your communities, whether that's in the North
of England, the South or South West, or Scotland, Wales or Northern
Ireland—or anywhere else in fact? The next chapter of this story lies with
whoever chooses to write it next.

Questions for reflection

1. Can you see places in your community where justice, reconciliation
   and forgiveness are happening, or where you can see the fruit of
   the Spirit?
2. How might God be working in these places?
3. How might you or your church join in with the work that's
   happening here?
4. Are the "trustees" of your church representative of the people in
   your community?
5. Are there ways that your church could give up some of its
   institutional power in its community?

Brief anonymized description
of the churches researched

We did some analysis of the relative poverty of our research parishes using the Church Urban Fund's database <https://cuf.org.uk/lookup-tool>. The rankings offered here were observed before our research visits and have changed slightly since (and so cannot be used to identify the churches). There are 12,382 parishes in England, and the lower the ranking, the poorer is the parish out of all that number. Readers will notice that *all* of our research churches were in the poorer 50 per cent of the total.

A—A Methodist church in Derbyshire. The church is in a town of c.11,000 people which had a history of mining. Rank: 1,567.

B—An Evangelical Anglican church in Lancashire. The church is in a town of c.15,000 people. The church was built in the Victorian era and was substantially reordered in the 1970s and 1980s. Rank: 5,663.

C—A new worshipping community in Yorkshire. Located in a town of 88,000 people, this church is made up of mainly homeless and vulnerable people. It meets in a Methodist church building, had an Anglican minister when we visited, and is supported by churches of all denominations. Rank: 1,186.

D—An Anglican church on a social-housing estate of a few thousand people in Lancashire. The church building closed in 2013/14, and the church now worships in a community centre. Rank: 297.

E—An Anglican church in Yorkshire. The church is located in a town of 138,000 people which had a history of mining. The church was built in the Victorian era, and was reordered and a community centre added recently. Rank: 2.

F—An Anglican benefice of five churches in rural Yorkshire. The five villages have a combined population of c.1,200. The data on these villages was too low to have a ranking in the look up tool.

G—An Ecumenical Team Ministry of three churches in a town in the North East. The town has a population of c.43,000 and a history of mining and shipbuilding. Of the three churches, one is a Victorian Anglican church, one is an Anglican/Methodist/URC church founded in the 1980s, and one is aVictorian Anglican church which has been converted recently into a chapel of ease. Rank: 1,423.

Bibliography

Andiñach, Pablo R. & Botta, Alejandro F. (2009), *The Bible and the Hermeneutics of Liberation* (Atlanta: Society of Biblical Literature).

Arendt, Hannah (1970), *On Violence* (London: Allen Lane, The Penguin Press).

Arnold, Malcolm (1869), *Culture and Anarchy* (London: Smith, Elder and Co).

Astley, Jeff (2002), *Ordinary Theology: Looking, Listening and Learning in Theology* (Aldershot: Ashgate).

Baker, Chris (2017), "Mission and Authenticity", *Anvil* 33:3 available online at <https://churchmissionsociety.org/sites/default/files/wysiwyg/Anvil_mission_aunthenticity_Volume_33_Issue_3.pdf>, accessed 23 August 2020.

Barker, Christopher (2011), *Cultural Studies: Theory and Practice,* 4th revised edition (London: Sage).

Barrett, Al (2020), *Interrupting the Church's Flow: A Radically Receptive Political Theology in the Urban Margins* (London: SCM Press).

Barrett, Al & Harley, Ruth (2020), *Being Interrupted: Reimagining the Church's Mission from the Outside, In* (London: SCM Press).

Bevans, Stephen B. (2002), *Models of Contextual Theology*, revised edition (Maryknoll, NY: Orbis Books).

Bevans, Stephen B. & Schroeder, Roger (2011), *Prophetic Dialogue: Reflections on Christian Mission Today* (Maryknoll, NY: Orbis Books).

Bickley, Paul (2018), *People, Place and Purpose: Churches and Neighbourhood Resilience in the North East* (London: Theos).

Boff, Leonardo & Boff, Clodovis (1987), *Introducing Liberation Theology* (Maryknoll, NY: Orbis Books).

Bosch, David J. (1991), *Transforming Mission: Paradigm Shifts in Theology of Mission* (Maryknoll, NY: Orbis Books).

Bradley, Ian (2017), book review of *Northern Gospel, Northern Church* in *Modern Believing* 58:2, pp. 207–208.

Brueggemann, Walter (1997), *Cadences of Home* (Louisville, KY: Westminster John Knox Press).

Brueggemann, Walter (2014), *Reality, Grief, Hope: Three Urgent Prophetic Tasks* (Grand Rapids, MI: Eerdmans).

Carson, Timothy, Fairhurst, Rosy, Rooms, Nigel & Withrow, Lisa (2021), *Crossing Thresholds: A Practical Theology of Liminality* (Cambridge: Lutterworth).

Casaldáliga, D. Pedro (1978), *Creio na Justiça e na Esperença* (Rio de Janeiro: Civilição Brasiliera).

Croatto, José Severino (1973), *Liberación y Libertad* (Buenos Aires: Ediciones Mundo Nuevo).

Crouch, Andy (2013), *Playing God: Redeeming the Gift of Power* (Downers Grove, IL: IVP Books).

Davey, Cyril (1985), *John Wesley and the Methodists* (Basingstoke: Marshall Pickering).

Davies, Rupert E. (1963), *Methodism* (Harmondsworth: Penguin).

Engelke, Matthew (2017), *Think Like an Anthropologist* (London: Pelican Books).

Eusebius (1945), "Vita Constantini" in *The Greek Ecclesiastical Historians of the first six centuries of the Christian Era* (London: Wertheimer).

Fox, Kathryn E. (2017), *Stand Up and Be (En)Countered: Resistance in solo stand-up performance by Northern English women, marginalised on the basis of gender, class and regional identity*, Unpublished PhD Thesis (Leeds: University of Leeds).

Frost, Michael (2006), *Exiles: Living Missionally in a Post-Christian Culture* (Peabody, MA: Hendrickson).

Gorringe, Timothy (1990), *Discerning Spirit: A Theology of Revelation* (London: SCM).

Gorringe, Timothy (2002), *A Theology of the Built Environment: Justice, Empowerment, Redemption* (Cambridge: Cambridge University Press).

Gorringe, Timothy (2004), *Furthering Humanity: A Theology of Culture* (Aldershot; Burlington, VT: Routledge).

Goto, Courtney T. (2018), *Taking on Practical Theology: The Idolization of Context and the Hope of Community* (Leiden; Boston: Brill).

Graham, Elaine, Walton, Heather & Ward, Frances (2005), *Theological Reflection: Methods* (London: SCM Press).

Green, Laurie (1987), *Power to the Powerless: Theology Brought to Life* (Basingstoke: Marshall Pickering).

Gutiérrez, Gustavo (1973), *A Theology of Liberation* (London: SCM Press).

Hall, Stuart (2018), "Notes on Deconstructing 'The Popular'" in John Storey (ed.), *Cultural Theory and Popular Culture: A Reader* (London; New York: Routledge).

Harper, Douglas (2002), "Talking about pictures: A case for photo elicitation", *Visual Studies* 17:1, pp. 13–26.

Heaney, Robert S. (2019), *Post-Colonial Theology: Finding God and Each Other Amidst the Hate* (Eugene, OR: Cascade).

Heath, Elaine (2017), *The Mystic Way of Evangelism: A Contemplative Vision for Christian Outreach,* 2nd edition (Grand Rapids, MI: Baker Academic).

Heifetz, Ronald A., Grashow, Alexander & Linsky, Marty (2009), *The Practice of Adaptive Leadership: Tools and Tactics for Changing Your Organization and the World* (Boston, MA: Harvard Business Review Press).

Hodgson, Janet (2018), *Mission from Below: Growing a Kingdom Community* (Durham: Sacristy Press).

Hopewell, James (1988), *Congregation: Stories and Structures* (London: SCM Press).

Hylson-Smith, Kenneth (1997), *The Churches in England from Elizabeth I to Elizabeth II: Vol. II, 1689–1833* (London: SCM Press).

Jewell, Helen (1994), *The North-South Divide: The Origins of Northern Consciousness in England* (Manchester: Manchester University Press).

Keifert, Patrick (1992), *Welcoming the Stranger: A Public Theology of Worship and Evangelism* (Minneapolis, MN: Fortress).

Kim, Kirsteen (2012), *Joining in with the Spirit: Connecting World Church and Local Mission* (London: SCM Press).

Kreider, Alan & Kreider, Elaine (2009), *Worship & Mission After Christendom* (Milton Keynes: Paternoster).

Lukes, Steven (2004), *Power: A Radical View* (Houndmills, Basingstoke: Palgrave).

Luther King Jr., Martin (2010 [1963]), *Strength to Love* (Minneapolis, MN: Fortress Press).

Lynch, William (1973), *Images of Faith: An Explanation of the Ironic Imagination* (Notre Dame, IN: Notre Dame University Press).

Marsh, Clive (2018), *A Cultural Theology of Salvation* (Oxford: Oxford University Press).

Methodist Church, The (n.d.), *The Methodist Quadrilateral*, retrieved from <https://www.methodist.org.uk/about-us/the-methodist-church/what-is-distinctive-about-methodism/the-methodist-quadrilateral/>, accessed 2 October 2020.

Milestone, Katie (2016), "'Northernness' gender and Manchester's creative industries", *Journal for Cultural Research* 20:1, pp. 45–59.

Newbigin, Lesslie (1995), *Proper Confidence: Faith, Doubt and Certainty in Christian Discipleship* (London: SPCK).

Niemandt, Nelus (2020), "The *Missio Dei* as Flourishing Life", *Ecclesial Futures* 1:1, pp. 11–30.

North, Philip (2016), "How the hills of the north are to rejoice" (*Church Times*) available online at <https://www.churchtimes.co.uk/articles/2016/29-april/books-arts/book-reviews/how-the-hills-of-the-north-are-to-rejoice>, accessed 3 March 2021.

Palmer, Parker (1981), *The Company of Strangers* (New York: Crossroad).

Pearmain, Rosalind (2007), "Evocative Cues and Presence: Relational Consciousness within Qualitative Research", *International Journal of Children's Spirituality* 12:1, pp. 75–82.

Pelikan, Jaroslav (1984), *The Vindication of Tradition: The 1983 Jefferson Lecture in the Humanities* (New Haven: Yale University Press).

Rack, Henry D. (2002), *Reasonable Enthusiast: John Wesley and the Rise of Methodism* (London: Epworth Press).

Reddie, Anthony (2009), *Is God Colour-blind? Insights from Black Theology for Christian Ministry* (London: SPCK).

Rich, Hannah (2020), *Growing Good: Growth, Social Action and Discipleship in the Church of England* (Theos/Church Urban Fund) available online at <https://www.theosthinktank.co.uk/research/2000/01/31/the-grace-project>, accessed 10 December 2020.

Rooms, Nigel (2012), "Paul as Practical Theologian: *Phronesis* in Philippians", *Practical Theology* 5:1, pp. 81–94.

Rooms, Nigel (2019), "Understanding Local Churches as Porous Living Systems: Insights from the Tavistock Tradition", *Ecclesial Practices* 6:2, pp. 182–197.

Rooms, Nigel & Keifert, Patrick (2019), *Spiritual Leadership in the Missional Church: A Systems Approach to Leadership as Cultivation*, L38 (Cambridge: Grove).

Russell, Dave (2004), *Looking North: Northern England and the National Imagination* (Manchester: Manchester University Press).

Schreiter, Robert J. (1985), *Constructing Local Theologies* (London: SCM Press).

Spencer, Stephen (2007), *SCM Studyguide: Christian Mission* (London: SCM Press).

Spencer, Stephen with Akiri, Mwita (2019), *Growing and Flourishing: The Ecology of Church Growth* (London: SCM Press).

Spracklen, Karl (2016), "Theorising northernness and northern culture: the north of England, northern Englishness, and sympathetic magic", *Journal for Cultural Research* 20:1, pp. 4–16.

Stone, Howard W. (2006), *How to Think Theologically* (Minneapolis: Fortress Press).

Sykes, Stephen (2006), *Power and Christian Theology* (London: Continuum).

Taylor, Charles (2018 [1991]), *The Ethics of Authenticity* (Cambridge, MA: Harvard University Press).

Wakefield, Gavin & Rooms, Nigel (eds) (2016), *Northern Gospel, Northern Church: Reflections on Identity and Mission* (Durham: Sacristy Press).

Walls, Andrew (1996), *The Missionary Movement in Christian History: Studies in the Transmission of Faith* (Maryknoll, NY: Orbis Books).

Weber, Hans-Ruedi (1989), *Power: Focus for a Biblical Theology* (Geneva: WCC Publications).

Whitworth, Patrick (2008), *Prepare for Exile: A New Spirituality and Mission for the Church* (London: SPCK).

Williams, Raymond (1981), *Culture* (London: Fontana Press).

Williams, Raymond (2014), *Keywords: A Vocabulary of Culture and Society*, 2nd edition (London: Fourth Estate).

Williams, Stuart Murray (2004), *Post-Christendom: Church and Mission in a Strange New World* (Milton Keynes: Paternoster).

Wort, Elli M. (2019), *Christian Theologies of Culture in Hull, City of Culture 2017*, Unpublished PhD Thesis (Leeds: Leeds Trinity University).

Wright, Christopher J. H. (2006), *The Mission of God: Unlocking the Bible's Grand Narrative* (Nottingham: IVP).

Index